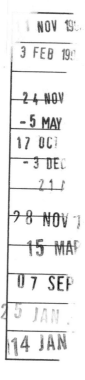

Shakespeare's Characters

A COMPLETE GUIDE

Cymbeline, Shakespeare calls up his name from the past, in French dress: Richard du Champ (Richard of the Field) - so like his subtle and oblique clues, the cast of his mind. One needs to be pretty subtle to uncover them: most of his commentators are unaware of them.

With regard to the historical characters - English, French, Roman and, occasionally Greek - I have identified them more clearly for the reader, and sometimes added a little information to clarify their careers. One hardly needs to identify characters like the English kings, or Julius Caesar, or Mark Antony and Cleopatra. But it may be helpful to point out that Shakespeare does not distinguish between the two dukes of Norfolk in the reign of Henry VIII, or that we are not always clear which Dauphin he is referring to, while he does distinguish Decius Brutus, Marcus Brutus, and Junius Brutus, as we should.

Generic names - gaolers, keepers, messengers, nurses, servants, murderers - are included only when they have something to the point to say.

> *the great traveller, and wild Halfcan that*
> *stabbed Pots, and I think forty more.*

No doubt he could have thought up forty more, if he had not gone on long enough already.

Names like Benvolio and Malvolio express character very well - the first of good will, the second of ill will. Though Malvolio is not a malevolent character, he certainly bears ill will to Sir Toby Belch and Sir Andrew Aguecheek - and how well they are named! - for their drunken roistering and keeping the household, for which he is responsible, awake all hours of the night.

The name Slender, for Shallow's cousin, may point to something further. Shakespeare's Company contained a notably lean and slender actor, one Sinkler or Sinclair. The entirely professional actor-dramatist kept the resources of the Company in mind in casting - and inevitably, to some extent, writing - his parts.

We come closer still to him with the names of the auto-biographically inspired *Love's Labour's Lost*. Don Adriano de Armado is very right for its easily recognisable caricature of Don Antonio Pérez, overstaying his welcome at this time at Essex House - the reference to the Armada obvious enough for Philip II's ex-Secretary of State. The Essex-Southampton group was well known to Henry of Navarre: Essex had met him in 1591, and Southampton's close friends, Sir Charles and Sir Henry Danvers, served under him in France. So it was appropriate for Shakespeare to annex the name of Navarre to do duty for Southampton in the play and use the names prominent in France at the time: Longueville, Biron, Mayenne. They all appear in the pamphlets which Shakespeare's fellow-townsman, Richard Field - himself married to a French widow - was producing in Blackfriars at the time. Remarkably, in a later play, facts, the difficulties and disappointments of Elizabethan recruiting, the names of Falstaff's musty recruits tell their own tale; though caricature, they are realistic enough - with one of them buying himself off: Mouldy, Shadow, Wart, Feeble, Bullcalf.

Other names suggest their occupations. What better than Fang and Snare, for sergeants of the law, sent to arrest culprits at the Boar's Head, or Dogberry for a constable, Costard for a clown? Those deleterious ladies, Doll Tearsheet and Mistress Overdone, are recognisably named, the one a whore, the other a brothel madam. Mopsa and Dorcas are pretty names for shepherdesses, Audrey right for a country girl. Shallow and Silence are good for country J.P.s, and so is Shallow's man, Davy, with his talk of shoeing and plough-irons, 'and a new link to the bucket must be had'. (When I first came to a country house with orchard in Cornwall, I had a man Davy, and his talk was much the same.)

A virtuoso passage in *Measure for Measure* shows what Shakespeare could do with names, when he chose, in a paragraph. Pompey - in itself a good name for a pimp - describes the fellows in gaol with him.

> *First, here's young Master Rash, he's in for a commodity of brown paper and old ginger, nine score and seventeen pounds, of which he made five marks ready money ... Then is there here one Master Caper, at the suit of Master Threepile the mercer, for some four suits of peach-coloured satin ... Then have we here young Dizzy, and young Master Deepvow, and Master Copperspur, and Master Starvelackey the rapier-and-dagger man, and young Dropheir that killed lusty Pudding, and Master Forthright the tilter, and brave Master Shoetie*

Introduction

George R. Stewart once wrote a delightful book, *Names on the Land*, an account of the naming of places in the United States, which showed how, in so vast a country, it was necessary to repeat names from state to state. Something of the sort happened in the world of Shakespeare's plays. Among several hundred names – in itself making it useful, if not necessary, to have a guide to them – more than a score are repeated, making it all the more necessary to distinguish between them, and providing a further argument for a convenient *Who's Who*.

Among the names he uses twice over we find the following: Angelo, Claudius, Cornelius, Diomedes, Emilia, Escalus, Flavius, Francisco, Gratiano, Helen, Helena, Juliet, Lucilius, Martius, Moth, Petruchio, Publius, Sebastian (both alike saved from shipwreck), Sempronius, Stephano, Varrius, Ventidius, Vincentio. Three times he uses the names Balthasar, Demetrius, Lucius, Titus, Valentine. And there are even five Antonios. It is necessary to distinguish between them, and as well to have a directory to them.

A glance at Shakespeare's naming of parts shows his instinctive tact at work. What could be more charming than the fairies in *A Midsummer Night's Dream* – Peaseblossom, Cobweb, Moth and Mustardseed? Or more appropriate than the country craftsmen who perform in the play of Nick Bottom the weaver – Peter Quince, a carpenter; Snug, a joiner; Francis Flute, a bellows-mender; Tom Snout, a tinker; Robin Starveling, a tailor? To anyone who knows the

First published in Great Britain 1984
by Methuen London Ltd
11 New Fetter Lane, London EC4P 4EE
Copyright © 1984 A.L. Rowse
Filmset in 10/12pt Compugraphic Century Textbook
by CK Typesetters Ltd., Sutton, Surrey
Printed in Great Britain
by Richard Clay (The Chaucer Press) Ltd
Bungay, Suffolk

British Library Cataloguing in Publication Data

Rowse, A.L.
  Shakespeare's characters.
  1. Shakespeare, William - Characters
  - Dictionaries
  I. Title
  822.3'3   PR2989

  ISBN 0-413-56710 9

A.L. ROWSE

Shakespeare's Characters

A COMPLETE GUIDE

METHUEN

Shakespeare's Characters

A COMPLETE GUIDE

Aaron the Moor, lover of Tamora, wife of the Emperor Saturninus, gives her a black bastard, and comes to a suitable end. *Titus Andronicus*.

Abbess, *Comedy of Errors, see* Aemilia.

Abbot of Westminster, *see* Westminster.

Abergavenny, lord, George Neville, 3rd baron, *c.* 1471-1535. *Henry VIII*.

Abhorson, an executioner, light if grim relief in *Measure for Measure*, a caricature but revealing of the time.

Abraham, servant to Montague. *Romeo and Juliet*.

Achilles, chief hero of the Greeks in the Trojan war

> *... whom opinion crowns*
> *The sinew and the forehand of our host.*

Over a dispute with Agamemnon about booty, he sulks in his tent with Patroclus; only when he is killed does Achilles rouse himself to do battle with Hector and kill him in turn.

There are flecks of Essex in Achilles: it was his habit to retire from Court and sulk in his tent whenever he could not get his way with Elizabeth I. He was saluted as an Achilles at the time. When Chapman published the second instalment of his translation of Homer's *Iliad* in

1598, he dedicated it to Essex as an Achilles of the age. Shakespeare made use of this work for his play. *Troilus and Cressida.*

Adam, faithful attendant on Orlando. *As You Like It.* An early tradition says that Shakespeare took this part.

Adrian (a) Neapolitan lord. *The Tempest.* (b) A Volscian in *Coriolanus.*

Adriana, wife of Antipholus of Ephesus. *The Comedy of Errors.*

Adriano, Don. *See* Armado.

Aediles, *Coriolanus.*

Aemilia, abbess at Ephesus, wife to Egeon. *The Comedy of Errors.*

Aemilius, a noble Roman. *Titus Andronicus. And see* Lepidus.

Aeneas, Trojan captain. *Troilus and Cressida.* Also a part assumed by the First Player in *Hamlet.*

Agamemnon, commander of the Greeks against Troy, the 'nerve and bone of Greece'. *Troilus and Cressida.*

Agrippa, M. Vipsanius, 63-12 BC, friend of Octavius, commander of his fleet at Actium. *Antony and Cleopatra. And see* Menenius.

Aguecheek, Sir Andrew, crony of Sir Toby Belch, gulled by him on the score of promoting his hopes of the Countess Olivia. *Twelfth Night.*

Ajax, Greek warrior in the Trojan war, portrayed as a blockhead in *Troilus and Cressida*. The play was written in 1602 at the time of the theatre-war - specifically referred to in *Hamlet* - when Ben Jonson attacked the Men's Companies, primarily Shakespeare's. The Cambridge skit, *The Return from Parnassus*, of just this year, alludes to it and adds, 'but our fellow Shakespeare hath given him a purge, that made him bewray his credit'.

The Prologue to *Troilus and Cressida* has a riposte to Jonson's 'prologue armed' Prologue:

> *A prologue armed - but not in confidence*
> *Of Author's pen, or Actor's voice, but suited*
> *In like conditions as our argument.*

That is, suited to the argument of the play, not the personalities of Author or Actor. And this is so like Shakespeare, unlike Jonson.

Others have thought Ben Jonson was pointed at in the description of Ajax: 'he is as valiant as the lion, churlish as the bear, slow as the elephant'. Jonson was notoriously slow in composition, Shakespeare equally rapid. 'A man into whom nature hath so crowded humours that his valour is crushed into folly, his folly sauced with discretion.' Jonson had made the line in 'humours' particularly his own.

Alarbus, son of Tamora, slain by Titus. *Titus Andronicus.*

Albany, duke of, married to Lear's daughter, Goneril. Has decent instincts towards her father - for which she despises him as a 'milk-livered man'. As her evil nature is borne in upon him he charges her,

> *Thou changed and self-covered thing, for*
> *shame*
> *Be-monster not thy feature.*

Though he calls her a 'fiend', her womanhood protects her from his hands. She retorts on him:

> *Marry, your manhood - mew!*   King Lear.

Alcibiades, c. BC 450-404. Only a sketch of this famous Athenian comes into *Timon of Athens*, for the play was unfinished.

Alençon, John, 2nd duke, 1409-1476, companion-at-arms of Joan of Arc. *1 Henry VI*.

Alexander (a) servant to Cressida, a Trojan, describes the characters of the Greeks to her, usefully at the play's beginning. *Troilus and Cressida*. (b) Alexander the Great, impersonated by Nathaniel, *Love's Labour's Lost*.

Alexas, Cleopatra's attendant. *Antony and Cleopatra*.

Alice, charming attendant who teaches Katharine of France English. *Henry V*.

Aliena, name assumed by Celia. *As You Like It*.

Alonso, king of Naples, wrecked on Prospero's island. *The Tempest*.

Amazons (a) warrior women in the masque. *Timon of Athens*. (b) *See* Hippolyta.

Ambassadors (a) from England, *Hamlet*. (b) From France, *Henry V*. (c) Antony's, *see* Schoolmaster. (d) From the Pope, *Henry VI*.

Amiens, lord attending on Duke Senior. *As You Like It*.

Ancient (i.e. Ensign), *see* Pistol, Iago.

Andromache, Hector's wife, who tries in vain to persuade him not to go forth to fight Achilles. *Troilus and Cressida.*

Andronicus, Marcus; and — Titus, *Titus Andronicus.*

Angelica, *see* Nurse.

Angelo, deputy for the Duke in *Measure for Measure*. A puritanical type, he imposes stricter sexual morals upon the city, condemning to death Isabella's brother for a lapse - which seems excessive to modern taste. He then seeks to seduce Isabella in return for her brother's life. She refuses - which again seems excessive to modern taste.

However, it enables Shakespeare to portray a hypocrite in full measure - a type with which he can have had no sympathy, from the conduct of his own life, and has none in the play, the whole subject of which is the exposure of Angelo.

Angelo, a goldsmith. *The Comedy of Errors.*

Angiers, citizen of. *King John.*

Angus, Scottish noble, returns with the English forces to overthrow Macbeth. *Macbeth.*

Anjou, *see* Reignier.

Anne (a) Richard III's queen, 1456-1485. Daughter and co-heiress of Warwick 'the king-maker', who betrothed her to Henry VI's son, the Prince of Wales, killed at Tewkesbury. She was then snapped up by Richard of Gloucester, who quarrelled with his brother Clarence

9

over her inheritance. She has a stronger part in the play than the poor woman had in life. *Richard III.* (b) *See* **Boleyn.** (c) *See* **Page.**

Antenor, Trojan captain, 'a shrewd wit'. *Troilus and Cressida.*

Anthony (a) servant to Capulet. *Romeo and Juliet.* (b) *See* **Dull.**

Antigonus, a lord of Sicilia. His comic 'Exit, pursued by a bear' has been regarded as improbable by people unacquainted with Elizabethan life. *The Winter's Tale.*

Antiochus, King of Antioch, who sets a riddle for the hand of his daughter (unnamed). Pericles guesses it to refer to the incestuous relations between father and daughter. (Shakespeare plays this down from the original story: he can have had no sympathy with that sort of thing, though tickling to a Jacobean audience.) In consequence Antiochus vows death upon Pericles, who escapes and is thus precipitated upon his course of adventures. *Pericles.*

Antipholus of Ephesus and **Antipholus** of Syracuse, twin brothers, sons of Egeon. The confusion of the two makes the fun of the play. Shakespeare made two characters instead of one in his source - an early exhibition of virtuosity. *The Comedy of Errors.*

Antium, citizen of. *Coriolanus.*

Antonio, brother of Leonato. *Much Ado About Nothing.*

Antonio, father of Proteus who is one of *The Two Gentlemen of Verona.*

Antonio, the Merchant. *See* Merchant.

Antonio, sea-captain, friend of Sebastian. *Twelfth Night.*

Antonio, usurping duke of Milan, Prospero's brother, shipwrecked on his island. *The Tempest.*

Antony, Marcus Antonius, c. 83 BC-AD 30, a close relation of Julius Caesar and his faithful follower. As consul he offered Caesar the kingly diadem at the festival of the Lupercalia, and he pronounced the panegyric over Caesar's dead body which is so effective in *Julius Caesar.* Antony and Caesar's heir Octavius finally defeated the republican party, led by Brutus and Cassius, at Philippi. Dividing the Roman world between them, Antony took the East; seduced by its glamour and falling under the spell of Cleopatra, Antony became more of an Oriental despot, to the disgust of the Romans. Octavius tried to effect a reconciliation, on the death of Antony's hostile wife Fulvia, by marrying him to his sister Octavia. But Antony tired of her and preferred the witchery of Cleopatra and the seduction of life in Egypt. Hence the tragedy of *Antony and Cleopatra.* Was the world well lost for love? Did Shakespeare think so? There is a shade of irony in his depiction and some rueful reminiscence of his own subjection to the tyranny of love in the spell exerted by a dark, inconstant, bewitching woman, unparalleled and alien, as was Cleopatra.

However, she gives him a magnificent epitaph in lyrical lines that bespeak her own love for him:

> *His legs bestrid the ocean ...*

and:

> *... his reared arm*
> *Crested the world, etc.*

Evidently he was great as lover, if not as leader, not a man to follow - though many did, as people will.

Apemantus, a 'churlish philosopher' in *Timon of Athens*, a cynic who serves as a clown, but really to bring home to Timon his folly: 'The middle of humanity thou never knewest, but the extremity of both ends.'

> *Thou hast cast away thyself, being like*
> *thyself:*
> *A madman so long, now a fool.*

Apothecary, in *Romeo and Juliet*, provides poison with which Romeo kills himself in Juliet's vault.

Apparitions, in the masque. *Cymbeline.*

Arc, Joan of. *See* Joan.

Archidamus, a lord of Bohemia. *The Winter's Tale.*

Ariel, a spirit at Prospero's command in *The Tempest*, one of Shakespeare's most imaginative creations. Ariel performs Prospero's magic behests, who promises him freedom at the end of his service. In the course of it he sings no less magical songs, 'Full fathom five', and 'Come unto these yellow sands'. In the latter, the words 'the wild waves whist' are Marlowe's, remembered from their close association years before.

Armado, Don Adriano de, a Spanish gentleman, made fun of in *Love's Labour's Lost*, is a recognisable caricature of Antonio Pérez, Philip II's exiled Secretary of State, at this time a guest at Essex House, well known to all the Southampton circle. His characteristics are clearly described by Navarre (Southampton): 'Our Court you know is haunted with a refined traveller of Spain', etc - his flattering rhetoric, boasting and lying. A well-known homosexual, he is laughed at in the play by being made to fall for a simple country wench.

This incontestable identification was made by Martin Hume, historian of Spain, at the beginning of this century, but has hardly even yet entered the closed minds of literary Shakespeareans.

Arragon (a) prince of, unsuccessful suitor to Portia. *The Merchant of Venice.* (b) *See* Pedro.

Artemidorus, a Sophist, has a schedule containing the names of the conspirators in *Julius Caesar.* The philosopher laments

> ... *that virtue cannot live*
> *Out of the teeth of emulation.*

He tries to present the paper to Caesar on his way to his doom, who says too grandly, out of a kind of bravado:

> *What touches us ourself shall be last served.*

Arthur of Brittany, 1187-1203, posthumous son of Henry II's son, Geoffrey, and Constance, heiress of Brittany. Since King John was the youngest of Henry II's sons, by primogeniture Arthur had a better right to the throne. Though only a boy, he constituted a threat to John, who, when Arthur fell into his hands, killed him, probably in a drunken fit in the castle at Rouen. Arthur has an appealing, pathetic part in *King John*; typically, to save the royal dignity, Shakespeare has him meet his end by leaping from the castle walls.

Arviragus, Cymbeline's second son in the play, brought up in Wales under the name of Cadwal, by the disguised Belarius. *Cymbeline.*

The two sons of the King refer to James I's two sons, Prince Henry and Prince Charles, as Imogen does to James's only daughter, Elizabeth. The play ends with a tribute to the new dynasty, the Stuarts, 'jointed to the old stock', i.e. the Tudors.

Asmath, a spirit raised by conjuration. *2 Henry VI.*

Astringer (medical attendant) to the sick King of France. *All's Well That Ends Well.*

Athenian, an old. *Timon of Athens.*

Athens, duke and duchess of. *See* Theseus, Hippolyta.

Audrey, a country girl. *As You Like It.*

Aufidius, *see* Tullus.

Aumerle (Aumale or Albemarle), Edward, duke of, d. 1415. Eldest son of Edmund, 1st duke of York; known earlier as earl of Rutland. Richard II made him duke. In 1399 he went over to Henry IV, but was deprived of his ducal title. Joining a conspiracy against Henry, he slipped out of it to make his peace, and succeeded his father as second duke of York. Killed at the battle of Agincourt, 1415. *Richard II.*

Austria, duke of, ally of Philip of France. *King John.*

Autolycus, a rogue on the roads, one of the most enchanting characters in all Shakespeare. Pretending to be a pedlar, attends the shepherds' feast to bemuse the maidens with his trifles, songs and ballads, to beguile and steal. *The Winter's Tale.*

Auvergne, countess of. *1* and *2 Henry VI.*

Bagot (Sir William), one of Richard II's agents. *Richard II.*

Balthasar, servant to Portia. *The Merchant of Venice.*

Balthasar, Romeo's servant, brings the mistaken news to Romeo at Mantua that Juliet is dead in her tomb at Verona. *Romeo and Juliet.*

Balthazar, a merchant. *The Comedy of Errors.*

Bandits, three, to whom Timon gives gold with such contempt that one of them says, 'He has almost charmed me from my profession, by persuading me to it.' *Timon of Athens.*

Banquo, supposed ancestor of the Stuarts, appears in *Macbeth* in compliment to James I. Banquo, along with Macbeth, sees the Witches, who foretell: 'Thou shalt get Kings, though thou be none.' A later tribute says:

> And to that dauntless temper of his mind
> He hath a wisdom that doth guide his valour
> To act in safety.

Because Macbeth fears him, and under him

> My Genius is rebuked, as it is said
> Mark Antony's was by Caesar,

Macbeth has him murdered.

In a later visit to the Witches, a show of eight Kings

15

appears, with the Ghost of Banquo, bearing a mirror,

> *Which shows me many more; and some I see*
> *That twofold balls and treble sceptres carry.*

This is a specific compliment to James I, king of England and Scotland, while the claim to France - the treble sceptre - was continued in the royal title until 1763.

Macbeth was conceived, in the winter of 1605-6, as a compliment to the new Scottish dynasty after the shock from the Gunpowder Plot in November 1605, with its threat to the royal family.

Baptista Minola (a) gentleman of Padua, who has two daughters to marry, one of them the unmanageable Kate the Shrew. *The Taming of the Shrew*. (b) *See* Gonzago.

Barde, Francis de. *Sir Thomas More*.

Bardolph, one of Falstaff's followers, distinguished by his red nose. *1* and *2 Henry IV, Henry V, The Merry Wives of Windsor*.

Bardolph, Thomas, 5th lord, 1368-1408, joined the Percies in revolt against Henry IV. Killed at Bramham Moor. *2 Henry IV*.

Barnardine, a condemned criminal in prison - really a grotesque, a caricature from contemporary life. Elizabethans found such types funny. In truth this play, *Measure for Measure*, always regarded as 'dark', a 'problem play', etc, has a great deal of comedy in it.

Barnardo, officer. *Hamlet*.

Bartholomew, a page. *The Taming of the Shrew*.

Bassanio, friend of Antonio, for whose debt to Shylock Antonio binds himself. *The Merchant of Venice.* The name Bassanio does not appear in the sources for the play. Was Shakespeare adapting the name from Bassano, so familiar to him from his experience with Emilia Lanier, born Bassano? The English pronounced the name Bassany, and often spelled it thus. It is thought that the Bassanos, or Bassani, were Italian Jews, which brings us even closer to the Italian-Jewish theme of the play. Evidently Shakespeare knew what he was writing about.

Basset, a Lancastrian. *1 Henry VI.*

Bassianus, brother of the Emperor Saturninus, loves Lavinia, Titus Andronicus's daughter, and is killed by Tamora's sons, who carry her off to rape and mutilate her. Hence Titus's ghastly revenge later. *Titus Andronicus* is a revenge play, of the type which Kyd patented - and Shakespeare, commencing author, went one better to pile horror upon horror and win popularity with this barbaric play.

Bastard, *see* Edmund, Faulconbridge, John (Don), Margarelon, Orleans, Thersites.

Bates, John, soldier in Henry V's army. *Henry V.*

Bawd (a) in *Pericles*, disappointed by Marina's strenuous defence of her virtue: 'Fie, fie upon her, she's able to freeze the god Priapus.' (b) *See also* Overdone.

Bear, a. *The Winter's Tale.*

Beatrice, niece to Leonato in *Much Ado About Nothing*, is of course intended from the first to fall in love with the convinced bachelor, Benedick. They begin with a suspicious dislike of each other, about which there is much ado, sparring with sharp repartees - very popular with sentimental Victorians, who all fell for Beatrice. A good deal of a minx, the best thing about her to our minds is her unquestioning loyalty to and belief in her cousin, the much-abused Hero.

Beaufort, Henry, cardinal, bishop of Winchester, d. 1447, son of John of Gaunt. Henry V named Beaufort guardian of the infant Henry VI, his great-nephew, whom he crowned king of France in Paris 1431. His prolonged conflict with his nephew, Humphry duke of Gloucester, for control of policy, where Beaufort favoured peace, provides much of the action of *1* and *2 Henry VI*. Never popular, Beaufort was a man of ability, diplomatic and administrative, particularly financial. He has his tomb and chantry in Winchester cathedral.

Beaufort, John. *See* Somerset.

Beaufort, Thomas. *See* Exeter.

Bedford, *see* John of Lancaster.

Bedlam, Tom o'. Character assumed by Edgar. *King Lear*.

Belarius in *Cymbeline* has been banished by the King, and in revenge abducts his two sons, who are presumed dead, but spirits them away to Wales, where he brings them up in the wilds as his own sons. He gives them the names of Polydore and Cadwal, himself going under the name of Morgan. He plays much the rôle of the Old Shepherd, who brings up the lost Princess, Perdita, as his daughter in *The Winter's Tale*. For Shakespeare was never averse to repeating himself, with a difference.

Belch, Sir Toby - what a good name for the roistering old uncle of the Countess Olivia, who keeps the house awake with drunken caterwauling. *Twelfth Night.*

Bellario, *see* Portia.

Benedick, a young lord of Padua in *Much Ado About Nothing.* Vowed to bachelordom, he for long resists the charms and sharp tongue of Beatrice. Their sparring and mutual banter - described as 'wit combats' by academic Shakespeareans - were mother's milk to Victorians. Perhaps less so to us; for of course they are obviously to be propelled into each other's arms by the intrigue of the play.

Benvolio, nephew of Montague, therefore cousin of Romeo in *Romeo and Juliet*: to whom it falls to console Romeo in his love griefs:

> *Alas, that love so gentle in his view,*
> *Should be so tyrannous and rough in proof.*

The name itself, as was often Shakespeare's way, indicates something of his character: good will.

Berkeley, attendant on Richard III's queen. *Richard III.*

Berkeley, Thomas, 5th lord, 1353-1417. *Richard II.*

Berowne (Biron), one of the lords attending on the King in *Love's Labour's Lost.* He regards the King's proposal to abstain from the company of women, to devote themselves to study, to be nonsense. His belief is that one learns life only through the love of women. Accordingly Berowne falls in love with Rosaline, who is described in closely similar language to the Dark Lady in the Sonnets (Emilia Lanier). Thus her description of Berowne,

> *a merrier man ...*
> *I never spent an hour's talk withal, etc*

is Shakespeare's recognisable skit on himself; as also his own characteristics are glanced at in his description of Berowne's in the first scene.

Berri, duke of. *Henry V.*

Bertram, Count, of *All's Well That Ends Well*, has an unsatisfactory character and yet is a significant figure in Shakespeare's work. He is a spoiled young aristocrat, with a charming mother, who refuses marriage - with Helena, the doctor's daughter in love with him. Made to marry her by the King, he flings off to Italy, where as Lieutenant-General of Horse, he performs a gallant exploit. The play continues his story.

But where have we met this character and situation before?

With young Southampton, whose patronage of and relationship with Shakespeare was decisive in his life. The spoiled young Earl refused marriage for years, until forced into it by his leader, Essex, whose cousin Elizabeth Vernon was far gone with child. The Earl had flung off to France. Next year, in Ireland as Lieutenant-General of Horse he performed a gallant exploit, though cashiered by the Queen - as Count Bertram was by the King in the play.

It was written in 1602, while Southampton was serving sentence in the Tower.

Betts, George. Shakespeare's scene in *Sir Thomas More.*

Betts, Ralph, clown. *Sir Thomas More.*

Bevis, one of Cade's rebels. *2 Henry VI.*

Bianca, Baptista's agreeable daughter, in contrast to the disagreeable Kate. *The Taming of the Shrew.*

Bianca, Cassio's mistress in *Othello*. Emilia, who is honest - as her husband, Iago, is not - calls her a strumpet. Bianca replies,

> *I am no strumpet, but of life as honest*
> *As you that thus abuse me.*

Be that as it may, she wears the handkerchief with its magic properties that Cassio has given her, and Othello recognises it as his own, confirming his suspicion that Cassio is his wife's lover.

Bigot (Bigod, Roger, 2nd earl of that family). *King John.*

Biondello, servant to Lucentio. *The Taming of the Shrew.*

Blanche of Castile, King John's niece, wife of Louis VIII of France. *King John.*

Blunt (Blount), supporter of the King, probably Sir John, knighted 1417. *2 Henry IV.*

Blunt (Blount), Sir James, d. 1493, knighted by Richmond, 1485. *Richard III.*

Blunt (Blount), Sir Walter, d. 1403, follower of John of Gaunt, killed at the battle of Shrewsbury. *1 Henry IV.*

Boatswain, a good stout fellow at the beginning and end of *The Tempest.*

Bohemia (a) king of, *see* Polixenes. (b) Prince of, *see* Florizel.

Boleyn, Anne, *see* Bullen.

Bolingbroke, a conjurer. *2 Henry VI.*

Bolingbroke, Henry, *see Henry IV.*

Bona, sister-in-law of Louis XI, proposed as wife for Edward IV. *3 Henry VI.*

Borachio, a follower of Don John, instrument of the frame-up against Hero to prevent her marriage to Claudio. *Much Ado About Nothing.*

Bordeaux, general of French forces. *1 Henry VI.*

Bottom, Nick, weaver, in *A Midsummer Night's Dream*, one of the most endearing of all Shakespeare's characters. He undertakes a play, with his fellow craftsmen, for the nuptials of the Duke. Their deplorable performance - a caricature of such provincial theatricals common in Elizabethan England - evokes the kindly comment from the Duke, which speaks for Shakespeare: 'The best in this kind are but shadows; and the worst are no worse if imagination amend them.' In the course of their comic rehearsals Bottom, falling victim to Puck's love-potion, is transformed into an ass. For of course he is a great ass. Shakespeare appreciated that lower-class people are often promising subjects for comedy.

Boult, servant to the Pandar in *Pericles*. Their realistic brothel-talk is convincingly contemporary, cf. my *Simon Forman: Sex and Society in Shakespeare's Age.*

Bourbon, (a) Admiral, *3 Henry VI.* (b) Duke of, Louis II, taken prisoner at Agincourt. *Henry V.*

Bourchier, Thomas, cardinal, archbishop of Canterbury, *c.* 1404-1486. *Richard III.*

Boy, a. *Much Ado About Nothing.*

Boyet, lord, attendant on the Princess of France. *Love's Labour's Lost.*

Brabant, Antoine de, duke of. *Henry V.*

Brabantio, Venetian senator, father of Desdemona in *Othello*. He is mortally offended by her marrying the Moor, deceiving her parent in doing so, and can only account for it by enchantment:

> *Damned as thou art, thou hast enchanted her -*

when she has already refused suitable Venetians of her own kind and race.

We can only conclude that the marriage did not take place under good auspices.

Brakenbury, Sir Robert, Lieutenant of the Tower, killed at Bosworth, 1485. *Richard III.*

Brandon, Charles, 1st duke of Suffolk, d. 1545. *Henry VIII.*

Brandon, Sir William, knighted by Richmond before Bosworth. *Richard III.*

Brentford, old Mother Prat of. *The Merry Wives of Windsor.*

Brewer, Robin. *Sir Thomas More.*

British captains, two. *Cymbeline.*

Brittany, duke of, John V. *Henry V.*

Brooke, name assumed by Ford. *The Merry Wives of Windsor.*

23

Brutus, Marcus. Of a Roman family famous for expelling the Tarquin kings, Brutus was brought up by his austere uncle, Cato, in aristocratic republican principles. Thus he fought for Pompey against Caesar, who pardoned him and treated him with favour and affection. In spite of this he was persuaded by Cassius to murder his benefactor. There was even a story in antiquity that Caesar had been the lover of Brutus's mother, and Brutus perhaps his son. But it does not need this to explain the bitterness of Caesar's last words, 'Et tu, Brute' - 'Thou too, Brutus.'

Brutus was adulated for virtue, but had the typical fault of the doctrinaire, lack of a sense of reality, let alone generosity or gratitude. In *Julius Caesar* Shakespeare gives him a better deal than he deserved historically: he portrays him as noble and virtuous, disinterested, entering upon the conspiracy out of republican principle, devoted to his wife and considerate of his slave-boy, Lucius. Upright and severe, with a moral superiority which gives him the leadership over others, he has the courage of a Stoic philosopher and will not allow himself to falter into grief even for his wife. He stands in contrast with the more human Cassius, with his failings.

And see Decius, Junius.

Buckingham, Edward Stafford, 3rd duke, 1478-1521. Executed on trumped-up charges, for his proximity to the throne, by Henry VIII. *Henry VIII.*

Buckingham, Henry Stafford, 2nd duke, 1455-1483. Supported Richard III's assuming the crown, but turned against him after his murder of the two Princes. Rose in rebellion, was captured and executed at Salisbury. *2 Henry VI* and *Richard III.*

Buckingham, Humphrey Stafford, 1st duke, 1402-1460. Supported Henry VI, opposed the duke of York, attempted to reconcile the two parties, but was killed at the battle of Northampton. *2 Henry VI.*

Bullcalf, Falstaff's Gloucestershire recruit. *2 Henry IV.*

Bullen (Boleyn), Anne, lady-in-waiting to Queen Katharine, afterwards Queen. *Henry VIII.*

Burgh, *see* Hubert.

Burgundy, duke of, in *Henry V*: John the Fearless, 1371-1419. His opponent the duke of Orléans was assassinated in 1407; himself assassinated in 1419. *Henry V* and *1 Henry VI.*

Burgundy, duke of, has an unchivalrous part in *King Lear.* Suitor for Cordelia's hand, when her father casts her off without dowry he concludes:

> *Election makes not up in such conditions.*

Bushy (Sir John Bussy), executed 1399. One of Richard II's agents, Speaker of the House of Commons. *Richard II.*

Butler, Ned. *Sir Thomas More.*

Butts, Dr, physician to the King. *Henry VIII.*

Cade, Jack, leader of rebellion, 1450. *2 Henry VI.* A caricature of a populist demagogue.

Cadwal, name assumed by Arviragus.

Caesar Julius, *c.* 100-44 BC, dominates the play of that name, as his personality was in Shakespeare's mind all his life. And that throws a revealing light on Shakespeare himself, for Caesar was the most variously gifted man in antiquity, the essence of whose nature was his ambition. The criticism has been made that *Julius Caesar* falls into two halves, because Caesar is assassinated in the middle. But his spirit continues to dominate the play - Shakespeare would know better than his critics.

To achieve dramatic balance he weakens Caesar's character, emphasises failings, in order to make out Brutus (with whom he cannot have sympathised) nobler than he was in historic fact. All the same, the impression of Caesar's greatness comes through, the sense that he was an exceptional being, easily able to dominate all who came near him, most of all at the moment of his murder.

Magnanimity (a characteristic Napoleon did not possess, nor Lenin, nor Stalin) was true of Caesar. Rumours of the conspiracy against him were all over Rome, yet he refused to be daunted - he had always lived dangerously. And clemency was one of his notable qualities: several of his assassins had received benefits and kindnesses from him. They could not forgive his astounding success, that he stood head and shoulders above other folk, or his popularity. An aristocrat, he always took the popular line, and was beloved of his troops and people alike.

So they struck him down, and civil war ensued.

And see Octavius.

Caithness, Scotch thane who returns with the English to overthrow Macbeth. *Macbeth.*

Caius, kinsman of Titus. *Titus Andronicus.*

Caius, name assumed by Kent. *King Lear.*

Caius (pronounced Keys), Doctor, French doctor who 'makes fritters of English'. *The Merry Wives of Windsor.*

Caius Lucius, general of the Roman forces in *Cymbeline*, who invade to exact the tribute to Augustus which the King has withheld. They land, improbably, at Milford Haven. Why? Because it was where Henry VII landed, James I's great-great-grandfather, through whom the throne had come to him. One compliment among several to James I in the Plays, never hitherto perceived.

Calchas, father of Cressida in *Troilus and Cressida* has a shifty little part in the intrigue of the play. A Trojan, he deserts Troy for the Greek camp, and proposes the release of Antenor in exchange for Cressida. Thus she comes over, transferring her 'favours' from Troilus to Diomedes. Like father, like daughter - a touch of the master which has gone unnoticed.

Caliban, slave to Prospero in *The Tempest*. The name is a pun on the word cannibal; he is the original inhabitant of the island, his mother a witch, himself half-monster and a savage. But he attempted to rape Prospero's daughter, for which he was enslaved. Shakespeare allows the pathos of the poor primitive:

> *When thou camest first*
> *Thou strok'dst me and made much of me;*
> *   would'st give me*
> *Water with berries in't; and teach me how*
> *To name the bigger light, and how the less*
> *That burn by day and night. And then I*
> *   loved thee,*
> *And showed thee all the qualities o' the isle,*
> *The fresh springs, brine pits, barren place*
> *   and fertile.*

This is exactly as it was with the first contacts between the Virginia colonists and the Indians, as we know from Hariot's *Brief and True Report*; cf. my *The Elizabethans and America*.

Calphurnia (Calpurnia), Julius Caesar's wife (his last historically), whose warnings of danger on the Ides of March he was at first inclined to listen to. It has been a night of storm, with fearful omens. She has the fine line,

> *The heavens themselves blaze forth the death*
> *   of princes.*

To which Caesar replies famously:

> *Cowards die many times before their deaths,*
> *The valiant never taste of death but once.*

Then he is overpersuaded by Decius Brutus, and goes to his doom. *Julius Caesar*.

Cambio, name assumed by Lucentio.

Cambridge, Richard, earl of, *c.* 1375-1415. Son of the 1st duke of York; brother-in-law of the earl of March, he fomented a silly conspiracy to place March on the throne, and was executed. *Henry V.*

Camillo, a lord faithful to Leontes's ill-used queen. *The Winter's Tale.*

Campeius (Campeggio), cardinal. *Henry VIII.*

Canidius, lieutenant-general to Antony. *Antony and Cleopatra.*

Canterbury, archbishop of, in *Henry V*, Henry Chichele, *c.* 1362–1443. Founder of All Souls College, Oxford. *See also* Bourchier, Cranmer, Warham.

Captain, (a) *Hamlet.* (b) *Macbeth.* (c) *King Lear.* (d) Roman, *Cymbeline.*

Captains, two British. *Cymbeline.*

Capucius, ambassador from Charles V. *Henry VIII.*

Capulet, head of his house, enemy of the Montagues, is quite peaceably inclined when young Romeo of the opposing house turns up at his feast. He is Juliet's father, and unkindly attempts to force her into marriage with Count Paris. Hence the tragic sequel. *Romeo and Juliet.*

Capulet, Lady, supports her husband in forcing marriage with Count Paris upon their daughter Juliet. She adds to this a virulent hatred of Romeo for killing her nephew Tybalt, a favourite with her. *Romeo and Juliet.*

Carlisle, bishop of, Thomas Merke, d. 1409. A faithful supporter of Richard II, protests against his deposition and foretells the troubles that would ensue. *Richard II.*

Carriers, two, make wonderfully convincing contemporary talk at the inn at Rochester. *1 Henry IV.*

Casca, 'the envious Casca', one of the conspirators against Julius Caesar. *Julius Caesar.*

Cassandra, a prophetess in *Troilus and Cressida*. She is the daughter of King Priam and therefore sister of all those foolish warriors. She prophesies the destruction of Troy, for the idiocy of a war over such an issue:

> *Our firebrand brother Paris burns us all.*

Dr Johnson was much impressed by her moral sentiment:

> *It is the purpose that makes strong the vow.*

Cassio, in *Othello*, is promoted by Othello as his lieutenant, though a Florentine, over the head of Iago, his ensign. Thus Iago means to ruin him, and does. He has no head for drink; Iago plies him with drink and involves him in a fracas with Montano and Roderigo. For this he is dismissed.

> *O I have lost my reputation, I have lost the immortal part of myself.*

To which Iago characteristically rejoins:

> *As I am an honest man, I had thought you had received some bodily wound: there is more sense in that than in reputation.*

Worse, Iago involves him in the destruction of Desdemona, who had known Cassio along with Othello.

Dr Johnson on him: 'Cassio is brave, benevolent and honest, ruined only by his want of stubbornness to resist an insidious invitation.'

Cassius, C. Cassius Longinus, an aristocrat who hated Caesar, patron and hero of the people. Cassius fought for Pompey against Caesar, who pardoned him; yet Cassius formed the conspiracy to murder the dictator and won over Brutus. At Philippi Brutus was winning on one wing of their army, while Cassius, defeated by Antony, committed suicide. Cassius was husband of Brutus's half-sister; he was able, but motivated by envy rather than principle. Nevertheless in the affecting scene before Philippi, in the dispute with Brutus, one cannot but feel that Cassius is in the right of it, though he yields to Brutus. *Julius Caesar.*

Catesby (a) *Sir Thomas More.* (b) Sir William, agent of Richard III, betrayed Hastings, d. 1485. *Richard III.*

Catling, Simon, musician. *Romeo and Juliet.*

Cato, *see* Young Cato.

Cawdor, Thane of. *See* Macbeth.

Celia, daughter of Duke Frederick, dear friend of Rosalind, the exiled Duke's daughter. *As You Like It.*

Ceres, goddess of harvest in the masque. *The Tempest.*

Cerimon, a lord of Ephesus. *Pericles.*

Chamberlain, Lord. *Henry VIII.*

Chancellor, Lord (Sir Thomas Audley, 1488-1544). *Henry VIII.*

Charles, wrestler to Duke Frederick. *As You Like It.*

Charles VI, of France. 1368-1422. His mental debility and incompetence as king exposed France to Henry V; but he had his revenge, for this was transmitted, through his daughter Katharine, whom Henry married, to his grandson Henry VI. *Henry V.*

Charles VII, of France, 1403-1461. Dauphin in *1 Henry VI*. In a victorious reign he recovered Henry V's conquests in France.

Charmian, Cleopatra's attendant in *Antony and Cleopatra*. She receives Cleopatra's confidences about Antony, and advises her,

> *In each thing give him way, cross him in nothing.*

To which Cleopatra rejoins:

> *Thou teachest like a fool - the way to lose him.*

She knows better how to hold Antony (as Emilia had Shakespeare; *see* the Sonnets). Faithful to the end, Charmian dies with Cleopatra, in the same manner, applying an asp to her breast.

Chatham, clerk of. *2 Henry VI.*

Chatillion, ambassador from France to King John. He fought at the battle of Bouvines, which put paid to John's Continental hopes. *King John.*

Chiron, one of Tamora's horrible sons. *Titus Andronicus.*

Cholmley, Sir Roger. Shakespeare's scene in *Sir Thomas More.*

Chorus (a) in *Henry V*, strikes a personal note, with contemporary references, especially in the Epilogue, where Shakespeare speaks in his own person:

Thus far, with rough and all unable pen
Our bending author hath pursued the story.

Opportunity should be taken to represent 'the bending author' as Chorus. (b) *Romeo and Juliet. See also* Rumour, Time.

Cicero, Marcus Tullius, 106-43 BC, senator, greatest of Roman orators and prose writers. He had attacked Mark Antony with vehemence in public speeches and so was marked down for proscription by him after Caesar's death. Caesar admired Cicero as a writer and would have liked to recruit him to his side; he was not privy to the conspiracy against Caesar, as the play *Julius Caesar* correctly shows us; but he approved of it. Shakespeare makes fun of his complacency and talking Greek - like an Englishman showing off his French.

Cimber, *see* Metellus.

Cinna, C. Cornelius, one of the conspiracy in *Julius Caesar.* Historically, he approved without joining it. Caesar had procured his recall from exile and made him praetor in the fatal year, 44 BC. But he remained an enemy, and after the assassination the mob nearly killed him.

Cinna, the poet in *Julius Caesar,* was the well-known poet, C. Helvius Cinna. Though walking in Caesar's funeral procession, he was mistaken for his namesake and murdered by the mob. Another poet makes an appearance in the play.

Citizen of Antium. *Coriolanus.*

Citizens, First, Second and Third, have a larger part in *Coriolanus* than any other play, for its subject is the conflict between an unbending heroic soldier and the mob. However, the First Citizen has a point: what

Coriolanus did for his country he did out of pride, and to please his dominating mother.

Citizens, of Rome, have a decisive part in *Julius Caesar*. They are rebuked by the Tribunes for so easily transferring their adulation of Pompey to Caesar. At Caesar's refusal of the crown, 'mere foolery', they hooted and 'threw up their sweaty nightcaps' - a contemporary Elizabethan touch. After his assassination, they applaud Brutus, completely misunderstanding his republican principles: 'Let him be Caesar', let him be crowned. They are then completely swayed by Mark Antony's appeal to their emotions, and turn round to slay the murderers and burn their houses, killing the wrong Cinna on the way. Never mind, 'tear him for his verses'.

Shakespeare, as a gentleman identifying himself with order, and a governing-class point of view, always depicts the masses as the fools they are, inconstant, fickle, credulous, cruel and merely destructive, open to any demagogue's appeal.

Clarence, George, duke of, 1449-1478. Brother of Edward IV, whom he deserted for Henry VI with Warwick, whose elder daughter he married, over whose inheritance he quarrelled with brother Richard. Done to death by brother Edward's orders in the Tower. *3 Henry VI* and *Richard III*.

Clarence, Thomas, duke of, *c.* 1388-1421, 2nd son of Henry IV; served under Henry V, killed at Beaugé. *2 Henry IV*.

Claudio, a young gentleman in *Measure for Measure*, condemned to death for getting his betrothed with child - an unsympathetic sentence to the modern mind. Still more unsympathetic is his sister Isabella's refusal to sacrifice her virtue to save his life. In the original source she did; in Shakespeare's play she would not. Why not? we wonder. Because it makes a better play, which was what concerned the experienced playwright. We may disregard the morass of ethical disquisition devoted to the matter.

Claudio, a young lord of Florence, is in love with Hero, but is the victim of a frame-up against her virtue by the villain, Don John. *Much Ado About Nothing.*

Claudius, Brutus's follower. *Julius Caesar.*

Claudius, King of Denmark, though he had murdered his brother to take his throne and is reviled by his nephew Hamlet, is not without regal qualities. He has the ability to rule, has royal dignity and the capacity to wassail with his courtiers, keep them in line drinking with them and providing sport - jousts, duels, wagers. (Those were barbarian times.)

But his crime ruins him: he is in so far he cannot but go on, cunningly plotting Hamlet's death. His conscience torments him:

> *O my offence is rank, it smells to heaven;*
> *It hath the primal eldest curse upon't,*
> *A brother's murder.*

Shakespeare's mind was haunted by Cain's crime in the Bible: here he made it the subject of his most moving tragedy. *Hamlet.*

Cleomenes, a lord of Sicilia. *Twelfth Night.*

Cleon, governor of Tharsus. *Pericles.*

Cleopatra, Queen of Egypt, 68-30 BC. The most famous woman in antiquity, a Macedonian Greek of extraordinary fascination for her beauty, vitality of spirit, intelligence, above all ambition. Caesar had supported her rule in Egypt and gave her a son, Caesarion. After his death she met Antony and conquered him, at twenty-eight. To seal reconciliation with Octavius Caesar, Antony returned to Rome to marry his sister Octavia. She could not hold his affection and he returned to his *femme fatale* in Egypt. In the ensuing war, Cleopatra's fleet retreated in the midst of the battle of Actium, hastening the loss of the day. She fled to Alexandria, where Antony joined her. Spreading reports of her death, she took refuge in her mausoleum. Antony stabbed himself in despair, but was drawn up into the erection to die in her arms. She could not effect the conquest of the wise Octavius, who meant only to carry her to Rome in triumph, where she was hated as an alien. So she ended her own life.

Shakespeare's portrait of her in *Antony and Cleopatra* is unparalleled in his work: she is unlike any other woman. Agatha Christie, a good Shakespearean of exceptional perception, saw that in recreating her he was remembering someone. The clue is that she is alien and different; mercurial in her moods, inconstant, ambitious, amoral, of exceptional vitality, above all betwitching. All these were characteristics of the dark, half-Italian young woman, Emilia Lanier, *née* Bassano - the Bassanos may have been Jewish - who had subjugated William Shakespeare.

Clerk, lawyer's, part assumed by Nerissa.

Clifford, John, 9th lord, 1435–1461. Defeated York at Wakefield and killed his young son; hence named 'the Butcher'. Killed at Ferrybridge. *2 Henry VI*, where his son also appears; and *3 Henry VI*.

Clitus, servant of Brutus. *Julius Caesar.*

Cloten, in *Cymbeline*, is the Queen's son by a former husband. She wants him to marry the King's daughter, Imogen, supposed heiress to the kingdom after the disappearance of her two brothers. Cloten pursues her with his boring attentions, 'whose love-suit hath been to me as fearful as a siege'.

For he is a boor; his name suggests 'clot' and 'clod', and he is both, a figure of fun. Dr Johnson criticised the character as wanting in consistency. But Shakespeare knew that human beings do not exemplify classic consistency, and that stupid people can sometimes talk sense. Cloten is patriotic, if boastfully so - 'We are a people such as mend upon the world'; but he is unwise in defying the Roman emissary demanding payment of tribute - this supplies the intrigue of the action, the sending troops to enforce it.

Cloten shows up badly in a game of bowls, is no sport when he loses, and comes to a comic end.

Clown, in *Antony and Cleopatra*. He brings the basket with the poisonous asps, with the wise remark, 'those that do die of it do seldom or never recover'. Shakespeare is not afraid to counterpoint comic with tragic, with strange effect, both relieving and heightening tension at such a moment.

Clown, in *Othello*, has a small part joking with the musicians employed by Cassio to bestir Desdemona.

Clown, has a small part in *Titus Andronicus*, thus early, to offset the horrors.

Clown, son of the old shepherd. *The Winter's Tale.*

Cobham, Eleanor. *See* Gloucester, duchess of.

Cobweb, a fairy. *A Midsummer Night's Dream.*

Coleville, Sir John, of the Dale. *2 Henry IV.*

Cominius, Coriolanus's companion-at-arms and general fighting with him against the Volscians: to whom Coriolanus addresses the most appealing lines he has in the play:

> *O let me clip [embrace] ye*
> *In arms as sound as when I wooed; in heart*

> *As merry as when our nuptial day was done,*
> *And tapers burned to bedward.*

May we not see Shakespeare's own experience in this? It is the way of real writers to be personal. *Coriolanus.*

Conrade, follower of Don John. *Much Ado About Nothing.*

Conspirators, with Aufidius. *Coriolanus.*

Constable of France. *Henry V.* He was Charles d'Albret, killed at Agincourt, 1415.

Constance, has an important part in *King John*, as bereaved mother of Arthur, the victim of political expediency ('Commodity'), and as a Cassandra foretelling woe. The heiress of Brittany, she married Henry II's son Geoffrey, elder brother of John; but Geoffrey died young, in Paris in 1186, and was buried in Notre Dame.

Cordellia, King Lear's youngest daughter, whom he throws off and disinherits because - put off by her sisters' hypocrisy - she will not flatter him with insincere adulation. She loves him, but will not go beyond what is due. This vein of obstinacy shows her her father's daughter. Actually he loved her best; as Goneril says, 'He always loved our sister most, and with what poor judgement he hath now cast her off appears too grossly.' True enough: hence her tragedy and his. *King Lear.*

Corin, a shepherd in the enchanting pastoral comedy, *As You Like It.*

Coriolanus, Caius Martius, hero of the play of his name, conferred upon him for his capture of Corioli. He is really a martial hero, but when persuaded to stand for civilian election to the consulship, his fault finds him out - his overweening pride and contempt for the people. The people's intuition tells them that 'he's a very dog to the commonalty'. Though persuaded to seek their votes, he will make no concession proper to the purpose. He knows them too well:

> *They'll sit by the fire, and presume to know*
> *What's done in the Capitol; who's like to rise,*
> *Who thrives, and who declines; side factions,*
> * and give out*
> *Conjectural marriages, making parties strong,*
> *And feebling such as stand not in their liking...*

We recognise the picture well enough today.

The tribunes of the people - perennial types of the demagogue - incite the mob against him; Coriolanus falls into the trap and tells them what he thinks of them. He is driven into exile with Rome's enemies, the Volscians, who give him command against his native city. He holds it at his mercy, rejecting plea after plea, until he succumbs to that of his mother and wife, and spares Rome. Returning to Volsci he is torn to pieces by the mob for his betrayal.

Coriolanus dominates the play singly and solely as no other, except Richard III. Shakespeare holds the dramatic balance here, giving the hero his due, while not sparing his faults; and something is to be said even for the people. On one side,

> *. . . where gentry, title, wisdom,*
> *Cannot conclude but by the yea and no*
> *Of general ignorance, it must omit*
> *Real necessities . . .*
> *Nothing is done to purpose.*

The word 'title' reveals that Shakespeare was thinking in contemporary, not Roman, terms.

On the other hand, the people have a case, and there is great dearth of corn to rouse them. This reflects the situation in Warwickshire and the Midlands, where there were agrarian risings in 1608, when the play was written. By this time Shakespeare - who always took a responsible governmental view - had himself become a landed gentleman.

Cornelius, courtier. *Hamlet*.

Cornelius, physician in *Cymbeline*, whom the wicked Queen employs to concoct a potion to poison Imogen. Instead he substitutes a sleeping draught, and all is well.

Cornwall, duke of, husband of Lear's daughter, Regan, in *King Lear*; is as evil as his wife in blinding Gloucester, though she has the more terrible line: 'Let him smell his way to Dover.' For his wicked action he is fatally stabbed by a servant who witnesses the deed.

Costard, clown. *Love's Labour's Lost*.

Court, Alexander, soldier in Henry V's army. *Henry V*.

Courtesan, a. *The Comedy of Errors*.

Cranmer, Thomas, 1489-1556, made archbishop of Canterbury to support Henry VIII's divorce from Queen Katharine. He supported Henry in all his doings, for which the King saved him from the malice of Bishop Gardiner and the conservatives - an historical episode which makes a scene in Henry VIII. At the baptism of Princess Elizabeth at the end of the play he is given a speech in the form of a prophecy, which constitutes Shakespeare's tribute to the great reign with which his own life coincided, with a further tribute to her successor, James I.

A Protestant martyr, burned under Katharine of Aragon's daughter, Queen Mary, Cranmer's best memorial is the Anglican Book of Common Prayer.

Cressida, niece of Pandarus in *Troilus and Cressida*, receives Troilus's ardent love with coy, bogus reluctance - she is willing enough. No fool, she realises that her uncle, the pandar, is but raising the young man's heat; and when he brings her a love token from Troilus, says,

By the same token, you are a bawd.

She is exchanged into the Greek camp, when she passes as easily and willingly, after a similar put-up show, into the hands of Diomedes. Troilus witnesses it, and is heart-broken.

She does not defend herself, any more than her virtue:

Troilus, farewell. One eye yet looks on thee;
But with my heart the other eye doth see.
Ah, poor our sex, this fault in us I find,
The error of our eye directs our mind.

Thersites draws the conclusion:

A proof of strength she could not publish
*   more -*
Unless she said, my mind is now turned
*   whore.*

Let us remember Shakespeare's rueful reproaches about the error of the eye leading the mind astray in the Sonnets, and his own personal experience of being deceived in love.

Cricket, a fairy. *A Midsummer Night's Dream.*

Crofts, *Sir Thomas More.*

Cromwell, Thomas, *c.* 1485-1540, son of a Putney brewer. He appears in *Henry VIII* as Cardinal Wolsey's faithful servant, which he was - his able agent in suppressing small monasteries to found Christ Church, Oxford. This set the pattern for the later Dissolution. Just before his fall - for his mistaken policy of alliance with German Protestants and promoting Henry's marriage with the unappetising Anne of Cleves - Cromwell was made Earl of Essex. Henry's execution of his ablest minister was unforgivable, but popular.

Cupid, god of love in the masque. *Timon of Athens*.

Curan, a courtier in *King Lear*, who brings news of the discord between Goneril and Regan.

Curio, gentleman attending on the Duke. *Twelfth Night*.

Curtis, servant to Petruchio. *The Taming of the Shrew*.

Cymbeline, King of Britain in the play of that name, from Cunobelinus, the historic British king (d. *c.* 40 AD), whom Shakespeare got, with some of the story, from Holinshed. He was contemporary with the Emperor Augustus, to whom he was a tributary. In the play he is kindly disposed, but impulsive, weak and ineffectual, in the hands of his wicked Queen.

The play ends with reconciliation all round and a graceful tribute to the new Stuart dynasty, James I, his two sons, the Princes Henry and Charles, and his popular daughter Elizabeth. An oracle reads: 'Whenas a lion's whelp shall, to himself unknown . . . be embraced by a piece of tender air; and when from a stately cedar shall be lopped branches, which - being dead many years - shall after revive, be jointed to the old stock and freshly grow . . . then shall Britain be fortunate and flourish in peace and plenty.'

So characteristic of Shakespeare's tact: 'the tender air' is the King's 'virtuous daughter' the Princess Elizabeth (from whom our present royal house descends). The 'lopped branches' of the play 'point thy two sons forth;'

> *The lofty cedar, royal Cymbeline,*
> *Personates thee . . . whose issue*
> *Promises Britain peace and plenty.*

James's reign, *Rex pacificus*, provided a long period of peace, after two decades of war.

And why, in the play, should the Roman forces land improbably at Milford Haven? Because that was where Henry VII, James's ancestor - the Stuarts 'being jointed to the old stock' - had landed.

Dardanius, servant of Brutus. *Julius Caesar.*

Dauphin, *see* Charles, Louis.

Davy, Justice Shallow's rustic servant. *2 Henry IV.*

Decius Brutus, conspirator against Caesar. He persuades Caesar to set forth against Calphurnia's warnings. *Julius Caesar.* He had served in Gaul under Caesar, who had promised him the government of Cisalpine Gaul (i.e. Northern Italy). Nevertheless he betrayed his benefactor. The year after he was put to death by Antony.

Deiphobus, one of King Priam's sons. *Troilus and Cressida.*

Demetrius, follower of Antony. *Antony and Cleopatra.*

Demetrius, in love with Hermia. *A Midsummer Night's Dream.*

Demetrius, one of Tamora's deplorable sons who rape and mutilate Titus's daughter, Lavinia. *Titus Andronicus.*

Dennis, servant to Oliver. *As You Like It.*

Denny, Sir Anthony, 1501-1549, rather a favourite with the capricious monarch. *Henry VIII.*

Derby, Thomas Stanley, 1st earl of, *c.* 1435-1504. Married to Henry VII's mother, he decided with his brother the issue at Bosworth. *Richard III.*

Dercetas, in *Antony and Cleopatra*, brought Octavius Caesar the news of Antony's death.

> *Mark Antony I served, who best was worthy*
> *Best to be served.*

Now he offers to serve Caesar - as Essex's followers went over to serve Robert Cecil. Such is politics, as Shakespeare well understood.

Desdemona, in *Othello*, is all purity and love, of utter devotion and obedience to her strange husband of another race, a Moor. So that her fate at his hand arouses utmost pity - the scene of her murder one of the most moving to compassion in all Shakespeare. The more so too that she cannot fathom why it has come upon her; she is so innocent that she does not understand unfaithfulness in a woman to her husband.

Dr Johnson says that, 'the soft simplicity of Desdemona, confident of merit and conscious of innocence, her artless perseverance in her suit [on behalf of Cassio], and her slowness to suspect that she can be suspected, are such proofs of Shakespeare's skill in human nature as, I suppose, it is vain to seek in any modern writer.'

What a tribute from such a source!

Perhaps we may dare to point out that she was not all that innocent in marrying Othello in the first place. It was not only without her father's consent - a serious breach of rule in those days - but utterly contrary to his wishes. He relinquished all interest in her, his farewell:

> *Look to her, Moor, if thou hast eyes to see:*
> *She has deceived her father, and may thee.*

This subtly prepares us for the tragedy of suspicion that is fiendishly prepared by Iago, of which both she and the Moor are victims, the murderer as well as the murdered.

Diana, daughter of a widow of Florence, whom Count Bertram wishes to seduce. *All's Well That Ends Well.*

Diana, goddess, appears at Ephesus. *Pericles.*

Dick, butcher, one of Cade's rebels. *2 Henry VI.*

Dighton. *Richard III.*

Diomedes, attendant on Cleopatra. *Antony and Cleopatra.*

Diomedes (a) *Antony and Cleopatra.* (b) Greek prince, to whom Cressida readily gives herself when exchanged into the Greek camp. *Troilus and Cressida.*

Dion, a lord of Sicilia. *The Winter's Tale.*

Dionyza, wicked wife of Cleon, governor of Tharsus, who arranges to have Marina murdered, but is frustrated of her intent. *Pericles.*

Doctor, in *King Lear,* is charged by Cordelia with the task of bringing her father round, in the French camp he has reached, after his trials and the loss of his reason. By means of sleep, and with the aid of music, Lear recovers his senses and is able to recognise the daughter he treated ill, in the most moving lines:

> *Pray do not mock me:*
> *I am a very foolish fond old man,*
> *Fourscore and upward ...*
> *... and to deal plainly,*
> *I fear I am not in my perfect mind.*

Doctor, English, in *Macbeth*, consulted as to Lady Macbeth's condition, concludes:

> *Were I away from Dunsinane, and clear,*
> *Profit again should hardly draw me near.*

Doctor, Scottish, in *Macbeth*, on Lady Macbeth's sleep-walking:

> *More needs she the divine than the physician.*

Dogberry, a constable in *Much Ado About Nothing*, a marvellous transcript from real Elizabethan life, spiced with caricature, malapropisms and all, in talk with his assistant Verges. It is through these wiseacres, constituting the watch and overhearing Borachio, that the plot against Hero is brought to light.

Dolabella, P., follower of Octavius. *Antony and Cleopatra*. After Caesar's assassination, Antony kept him in line, awarding him the province of Syria. There Cassius besieged him in Laodicea; on its fall Dolabella ordered one of his soldiers to kill him.

Doll (a) *see* Tearsheet. (b) Williamson's wife. *Sir Thomas More*.

Donalbain, son of King Duncan in Macbeth. After the King's murder, his son Malcolm flies to England, Donalbain to Ireland and is naturally not heard of again. *Macbeth*.

Don John, bastard brother of Don Pedro: the villain of the piece, he attempts a frame-up against Hero, affianced to Claudio. *Much Ado About Nothing*.

Don Pedro, Prince of Arragon. *Much Ado About Nothing*.

Doorkeeper, to the Council Chamber. *Henry VIII*.

Dorcas, shepherdess. *The Winter's Tale*.

Doricles, name assumed by Florizel. *The Winter's Tale*.

Dorset, Thomas Grey, 1st marquis, 1451-1501. Son of Edward IV's queen, Elizabeth Woodville, by her first husband. Opponent of Richard III, joined Richmond in exile. *Richard III*.

Douglas, Archibald, 4th earl, *c.* 1369-1424. Fought against Henry IV at Shrewsbury, taken prisoner and ransomed. Slain at Verneuil. *1 Henry IV*.

Downes, Nicholas. *Sir Thomas More*.

Duke, the, in *Measure for Measure*, is Vincentio, duke of Vienna. He retires for a while, to watch, disguised as a friar, the operation of his government, which has become somewhat lax. He leaves as his Deputy the strict Angelo. This sets going the action, with which he remains in touch in disguise; he reveals himself at the end to distribute justice all round.

Duke Frederick, brother of Duke Senior whose dukedom he usurped. *As You Like It*.

Duke Senior, in exile in the Forest of Arden. *As You Like It*.

Duke of Venice - summons Othello urgently to take command in Cyprus against the Turks. In the course of the session Desdemona's father arrives to protest against Othello's marrying his daughter. The Duke sagely advises:

> To mourn a mischief that is past and gone
> Is the next way to draw new mischief on.
> > *Othello*.

Dull, a constable. *Love's Labour's Lost.*

Dumain, captain. *All's Well That Ends Well.*

Dumaine (i.e. Mayenne), French lord attendant on Navarre. *Love's Labour's Lost.*

Duncan, King of Scotland, whom Macbeth murders to take his throne. In *Macbeth* Duncan is truly regal, kindly and generous, and rewards Macbeth's service by making him Thane of Cawdor. He condescends to lodge for the night under Macbeth's roof - so that apart from murder, the deed is, as Macbeth realises, a shocking breach of the Celtic custom of hospitality.

Historically, it seems that Duncan was not all that guileless, and perhaps Macbeth not all that guilty. For Celtic custom ruling the succession to the throne was dubious and frequently contested; and it appears that Macbeth's reign was satisfactory enough, as things went.

Dutch Gentleman, a. *Cymbeline.*

Edgar, in *King Lear*, is the legitimate son of Gloucester, whose mind is poisoned against him by his bastard brother, Edmund. His life in danger, he escapes the Court and wanders, disguised as a vagrant, in the crazy following of the King across heath and wild. Thus he meets his blinded father also on the way, but does not make himself known until he saves his father from intended suicide. Encountering his evil brother he kills him in fair fight.

At the end of all, when Albany commands him as a young man, to

> *Rule in this realm, and the gored state*
> *sustain . . .*

he accepts:

> *The weight of this sad time we must obey.*

Edmund, the bastard son of Gloucester in *King Lear* is a whole-hearted villain. He invents lying charges against his brother Edgar to turn their father's mind against him and endanger his life. He lends himself to the purposes of Goneril and Regan, both of whom are in love with him:

> *To both these sisters have I sworn my love:*
> *Each jealous of the other, as the stung*
> *Are of the adder. Which of them shall I take?*
> *Both? One? Or neither? Neither can be*
> *enjoyed,*
> *If both remain alive.*

49

In the event, all three get their deserts, Edmund appropriately at the hand of the brother he had wronged.

Edward IV, 1442-1483, son of Richard, 3rd duke of York. Handsome and energetic, his military ability defeated the Lancastrians, and enabled him to take Henry VI's place as king. He privately married Elizabeth Woodville, thus alienating Warwick, who went over with Edward's brother, Clarence, to the Lancastrians and restored Henry VI. In 1471 Edward returned, defeated Warwick at Barnet, and Queen Margaret at Tewkesbury, and resumed the throne. In 1478 Edward imprisoned his disloyal brother, Clarence, in the Tower and had him done away with. Edward's early death precipitated the crisis which led to his brother Gloucester's *coup d'état* and seizure of his nephew's throne. These events are rendered, mainly from Holinshed's Chronicles and Hall's History, in *2* and *3 Henry VI*, and *Richard III*.

Edward V, 1470-1483, elder son of Edward IV. On his father's premature death Edward was being conducted from Wales to London when he was intercepted by his uncle Gloucester, who at first recognised him as king, then usurped his throne and had him murdered with his brother in the Tower. *Richard III*.

Edward, Prince of Wales, 1453-1471, son of Henry VI, killed after Tewkesbury. *3 Henry VI*.

Egeon, merchant of Syracuse. *The Comedy of Errors*.

Egeus, father to Hermia. *A Midsummer Night's Dream*.

Eglamour, gentleman of Milan, suitor for the hand of Silvia. *The Two Gentlemen of Verona*.

Elbow, a constable, whose lower-class speech provides light relief in *Measure for Measure*.

Elinor, *c.* 1122-1204, Henry II's queen, mother of Richard Coeur-de-lion, Geoffrey, King John and others. Heiress of Aquitaine, she was first married to Louis VII of France, from whom she was divorced to marry Henry II. She took her full share in the quarrels of Henry and his tempestuous sons, but ultimately supported John as king, against Anjou which declared for Geoffrey's son, Arthur. She is buried in Fontévraud abbey, where one sees her tomb along with Coeur-de-lion: at rest at last. *King John.*

Elizabeth, Edward IV's queen, *c.* 1437-1492, widow of Sir John Grey. Petitioning Edward IV for the restitution of her husband's forfeited lands, she effected his conquest, who privately married her, and had her crowned 1465. She advanced her family which, talented and ambitious, was unpopular. On Edward's death, she took sanctuary in Westminster Abbey to protect her younger son, but was forced to surrender him to Richard. After the murder of her sons Richard III was prevented from marrying their sister, thus heiress of York, whose marriage to Henry VII healed the breach between York and Lancaster. *3 Henry VI* and *Richard III.*

Elizabeth I, 1533-1603, daughter of Henry VIII and Queen Anne (Boleyn), born at Greenwich. She has a non-speaking part as an infant at her baptism by Archbishop Cranmer, whose prophetic speech at the event gave Shakespeare the opportunity to pronounce a panegyric on her reign, and a promising forecast for James I - thus rounding off his own life's work. *Henry VIII.*

Ely, bishop of, in *Henry V.* John Fordham was bishop 1388-1425.

Ely, bishop of, in *Richard III. See* Morton.

51

Emilia, lady attending on Queen Hermione. *The Winter's Tale.*

Emilia, in *Othello*, is the wife of the wicked Iago, the depth of whose villainy she does not penetrate. She is given the task of looking after Desdemona, to whom she is loyal; but, such is life's irony, that she becomes a means of Desdemona's destruction, through handing Othello's sacramental handkerchief, which she picks up, to Iago, who gives it to Cassio with evil intent, and he gives it to his mistress Bianca. Thus is Desdemona betrayed.

Emilia is all woman, of kind heart but no superior virtue. In the wonderful scene of her preparing Desdemona for bed - which proves her death-bed - Desdemona is unable to understand women being unfaithful to their husbands:

> *Woulds't thou do such a deed for all the world?*

To which Emilia:

> *The world's a huge thing; it is a great price for a small vice.*

Dr Johnson says, 'even the inferior characters of this play would be very conspicuous in any other piece, not only for their justness but their strength'.

Enobarbus (Ahenobarbus), Cn. Domitius, has a part of some pathos in *Antony and Cleopatra*. Shakespeare treats his change of sides and desertion of Antony more sympathetically than history warrants - his ambivalence evidently appealed to Shakespeare. Actually Ahenobarbus was one of those pardoned by Caesar for fighting for Pompey against him. After Caesar's death Ahenobarbus commanded the republican fleet in the Aegean, but became reconciled to Antony. He then went back on Antony and deserted him. Generous as ever, Antony sent his treasure after him:

> *Thou mine of bounty, how wouldst thou have*
> *paid*
> *My better service ...*

Unable to bear the strain upon his conscience, he dies.

Ephesus, Solinus, duke of. *The Comedy of Errors.*

Erasmus. *Sir Thomas More.*

Eros, friend of Antony. *Antony and Cleopatra.*

Erpingham, Sir Thomas, 1357-1428, follower of John of
Gaunt, Henry IV and Henry V, took part as an elderly
man at Agincourt. Commemorated by the Erpingham
Gate at Norwich. *Henry V.*

Escalus, an old lord in *Measure for Measure.* He is faithful
to the absenting Duke and helps his Deputy meanwhile
to govern. But he is more kindly disposed to men's
failings, and expresses the Shakespearean sentiment:

> *Well, Heaven forgive him [the condemned*
> *Claudio], and forgive us all.*
> *Some rise by sin, and some by virtue fall.*

(Even this has a bawdy innuendo - 'rise' and 'fall' - so
like Shakespeare.)

Escalus, Prince of Verona, denounces the feud between
Montague and Capulet that leads to brawls in the
streets. It falls to him to banish Romeo, in *Romeo and
Juliet*, for killing Tybalt in another such affray. After the
tragic events of the play he sums up:

> *Where be these enemies? Capulet, Montague,*
> *See what a scourge is laid upon your hate,*
> *That heaven finds means to kill your joys*
> *with love.*

53

> *And I, for winking at your discords too,*
> *Have lost a brace of kinsmen - all are*
> *punished.*

Escanes, a lord of Tyre. *Pericles*.

Essex, Geoffrey FitzPeter, earl, d. 1215. *King John*.

Evans, Sir Hugh, Welsh curate, whose comic accent is made fun of in *The Merry Wives of Windsor*.

Exeter, (a) Thomas Beaufort, duke of, d. 1427. Youngest son of John of Gaunt by Catherine Swinford, took a prominent part in Henry V's war in France, appointed by him guardian of the infant Henry VI. *Henry V, 1 Henry VI*. (b) Henry Hollard, duke of, *3 Henry VI*.

Exton, Sir Piers, unknown to history, supposed murderer of Richard II at Pontefract Castle. *Richard II*.

Fabian, servant to the Countess Olivia. *Twelfth Night*.

Falstaff, Sir John, Shakespeare's greatest comic creation. He had originally called him Oldcastle, after the original Lollard knight, but this was objected to by the Cobhams, representatives of Oldcastle's wife's family. Falstaff has a dominant rôle as a crony of Prince Henry, but is discountenanced by him, rightly, on becoming king. All this occupies much of *1* and *2 Henry IV*; his end is described at the beginning of *Henry V*. He was revived at the express command of Queen Elizabeth I, who wished to see 'Sir John in love'; hence *The Merry Wives of Windsor*, which he entirely dominates and where his amorous propensities are exposed and get their come-uppance.

It has not been observed that there is an element of Shakespeare himself in this most intimate creation, not least in his wit and merriment, his sheer verbal virtuosity. And sometimes the character expresses what his creator thought, e.g. about 'honour'. Neither Falstaff nor Shakespeare was one to risk life for 'honour', like the fighting fools; or, for that matter, Marlowe, Ben Jonson, or other duelling dramatists.

No wonder Falstaff is a lovable creation, for all his roguery: pre-eminently one of those characters – Dr Johnson observed – which the author delighted to depict.

In *2 Henry IV* Falstaff's page appears.

Fang – suitably named, sergeant of the law. *2 Henry IV*.

Fastolfe, Sir John, *c*. 1378-1459, knighted 1427; made his fortune fighting in France; held many commands, was groundlessly accused of cowardice (this may have given a tip for the character of Falstaff later) at Patay. Built Caistor Castle with his gains; prominent in the *Paston Letters. 1 Henry VI.*

Father, that has killed his son. *3 Henry VI.*

Faulconbridge, Philip, the Bastard, supposed son of Richard Coeur-de-lion in *King John*, and the play's most original character, an invention of Shakespeare, through whom he expresses his views, e.g. on Commodity, i.e. political expediency.

Faulconbridge, Robert, legitimate son of Sir Robert, Shakespeare's invention. So too Lady Faulconbridge, mother of both Robert and Philip. *King John.*

Feeble, Francis, one of Falstaff's recruits. *2 Henry IV.*

Fenton, a young gentleman, in love with Anne Page and marries her at Eton. *The Merry Wives of Windsor.*

Ferdinand (a) son of the king of Naples, shipwrecked on Prospero's island; intended from the first to fall in love with his daughter, and make a happy ending. *The Tempest.* (b) King of Navarre, *Love's Labour's Lost*, a friendly, courteous skit on Southampton by his poet and friend, the actor-dramatist of the circle.

Feste, jester to the Countess Olivia in *Twelfth Night*, has the lovely songs to sing, 'Come away, come away, death', and 'When that I was and a little tiny boy'.

Fidele, name assumed by Imogen.

Fiends, appear to Joan of Arc. *1 Henry VI.*

Fishermen. *Pericles.*

Fitzwater, lord. *Richard II.* This would be Walter, 5th lord, 1368-1406. Walter was earlier pronounced Water, without the 'l'.

Flaminius, servant to Timon. *Timon of Athens.*

Flavius, servant to Brutus. *Julius Caesar.*

Flavius, a tribune of the people, hostile to Caesar. *Julius Caesar.*

Flavius, Timon's faithful steward, in *Timon of Athens*, the most sympathetic figure in the play. Driven to his wits' end to raise money to meet Timon's extravagance and pay his debts, he offers his own savings to relieve the misery his master is reduced to. He reflects:

> *Who would not wish to be from wealth*
> *exempt,*
> *Since riches point to misery and contempt?*

Thus Timon exempts him singly from his curse upon mankind:

> *It almost turns my dangerous nature mild.*

Fleance, son of Banquo, who escapes when his father is murdered. *Macbeth.*

Florence, duke of. *All's Well That Ends Well.*

Florizel, Prince of Bohemia, who is romantically destined for the fair Perdita in *The Winter's Tale*. (This rare name turned up in Shakespeare's time in Warwickshire.)

Fluellen (i.e. Llewelyn), gallant Welsh captain in Henry V's army, whose speech is made much fun of. *Henry V*.

Flute, Francis, bellows-mender. *A Midsummer Night's Dream*.

Fool (a) in *King Lear* has the most important part for a jester in the whole of Shakespeare, almost a philosophic part, played by Robert Armin, the remarkable comedian of the Company who succeeded Will Kemp. Where Kemp was a boisterous extrovert, Armin was reflective and, like many famous clowns, given to melancholy, a writer in his own right.

The Fool's rôle is the important one of counterpointing the King's folly, helping to bring him to his senses. He can tell the King why the snail has a house: 'Why, to put's head in: not to give it away to his daughters, and leave his horns without a case.' What a fool indeed Lear has been! - 'Thou shouldst not have been old, till thou hadst been wise.'

To which the King replies pathetically, in the famous line:

> *O let me not be mad, not mad, sweet heaven!*

But he is driven mad. In the tempest when they take refuge in a hovel - the King, his Fool, Edgar disguised as Mad Tom - there ensues a phantasmagoria of clever craziness, one of the most extraordinary scenes in literature. (Positively Russian - it might be Dostoievsky.)

(b) Fool in *Timon of Athens*.

Ford, Frank, townsman of Windsor, in *The Merry Wives of Windsor*, jealous of his wife's honour, disguises himself as Master Brook, encouraging Sir John Falstaff's addresses to test it. Both Falstaff and Ford are amusingly caught out and farcically shown up.

Ford, Mistress, Ford's wife whose honour remains untarnished throughout Falstaff's battering siege, and both men made fools of. *The Merry Wives of Windsor*.

Forester, a. *Love's Labour's Lost*.

Forrest, *Richard III*.

Fortinbras, prince of Norway. *Hamlet*.

France, King of, whose sickness and its cure by Helena set going the action. *All's Well That Ends Well*. His active disapproval of Count Bertram echoes Elizabeth I's disapproval of Southampton.

France, King of, in *King Lear* is a pattern of chivalry. When Cordelia is turned off by her father, and turned down by Burgundy, the king of France accepts her and marries her without conditions or dower. When they return to England to rescue Lear and put things to rights, they are defeated, Cordelia is captured and hanged in prison. Goneril and Edmund gave the order.

This dreadful *dénouement* - which the tender heart of Dr Johnson could not bear to think of - was not in the original version of the Lear story. It was the extremism of Shakespeare's imagination that led him to wring our hearts unbearably with this. He could confront the worst horrors in life - as we hardly can those in our time on a vaster scale.

And see Charles, Louis.

France, the Princess of, whose irruption upon the scene with her ladies disrupts Navarre's intention of abstaining from women's company to devote himself and his courtiers to study. *Love's Labour's Lost*.

And see Katharine.

Francis, a drawer at the Boar's Head in East Cheap, who is made fun of by Prince Henry and his deleterious companions. *1* and *2 Henry IV*.
And see Friar Francis.

Francisca, a nun. *Measure for Measure*.

Francisco, a Neapolitan lord. *The Tempest*.

Francisco, an officer. *Hamlet*.

Frederick, Duke, usurper of his brother's dukedom. *As You Like It*.

French gentleman, in *Cymbeline*. He meets Leonatus Posthumus again in Rome, and raises –characteristically for a Frenchman - the contentious subject of the chastity, or virtue, of 'our country mistresses'. Leonatus unfortunately takes the wager to put his wife, Imogen's, to the proof - fortunately for us, or there would have been no sub-plot to the play.

French lords, two. *All's Well That Ends Well*.

Friar Francis, in *Much Ado About Nothing*, defends the much-abused Hero, and in giving advice has some notably beautiful lines to speak.

Friar John is Friar Laurence's *confrère*, who fails to deliver the latter's letter from Verona to Romeo - hence the fatality of his not knowing that Juliet's death was only presumed, not dead in fact. The reason? - the friars

> Sealed up the doors, and would not let us forth
> Where the infectious pestilence did reign.

Remember that the years 1592 and 1593 were plague

years, the theatres closed for most of the period, and the pestilence much in mind at the time. This failure to communicate led to the catastrophe at the end of *Romeo and Juliet*.

Friar Laurence has an important part in *Romeo and Juliet*, for he is the confidant of the lovers - indeed Juliet's confessor - and secretly marries them. He shelters Romeo in his cell after the killing of Tybalt. When Juliet is faced with the immediate threat of going through a marriage ceremony with Count Paris, the Friar suggests a means of escape - which ends, however, fatally.

Friar Peter. *Measure for Measure.*

Friar Thomas, supplies the Duke with his disguise as a friar. *Measure for Measure.*

Froth, a gentleman of no importance. *Measure for Measure.*

Gabriel, a servant mentioned in *The Taming of the Shrew*.

Gadshill, a robber on the road. *1 Henry IV*.

Gallus, C. Cornelius, friend of Octavius. *Antony and Cleopatra*. At Actium he commanded a detachment of the army, and then was sent in pursuit of Antony to Egypt.

Ganymede, name assumed by Rosalind.

Gaoler (a) *Comedy of Errors*. (b) *The Merchant of Venice*. (c) Mortimer's. *1 Henry VI*.

Gaoler of Queen Hermione. *The Winter's Tale*.

Gaolers, two, in charge of Leonatus on his return from exile, given the characteristic talk of such wiseacres. *Cymbeline*.

Gardener, a, in *Richard II*, holds converse with the Queen.

Gardiner, Stephen, bishop of Winchester, *c.* 1483-1555, tries to bring archbishop Cranmer down in *Henry VIII*.

Gargrave, Sir Thomas. *1 Henry VI*.

Garter King-at-arms. *Henry VIII*.

Gascoigne, Sir William. *See* Lord Chief Justice.

Gaunt (i.e. Ghent), John of, duke of Lancaster, 1340-1399, 4th son of Edward III. Had a long military career fighting in France and Spain. In England he attempted to guide his young nephew, Richard II, but sometimes was in opposition. Eventually he married his mistress Catherine Swinford, and their children, the Beauforts, were legitimised by Parliament. With his first wife Blanche of Lancaster he acquired her vast inheritance. Patron of the arts, his splendid collections at the Savoy were sacked in the Peasants' Revolt, 1381; his magnificent tomb in Old St Paul's was destroyed during the Puritan Commonwealth. In his last years Gaunt tried to hold the royal family together but, his health failing, Richard II went his own wilful way to destruction, more or less as depicted in the play. *Richard II*.

General, a French. *1 Henry VI*.

Gentleman, attendant on Cordelia. *King Lear*.

Gentleman, a courtier in *Hamlet*.

Gentlemen, First and Second. *All's Well That Ends Well*.

Gentlemen, two, appear in the first scene of *Cymbeline*, to explain the situation at Court from which the play proceeds.

Gentlemen, three, in *Henry VIII*, describe Anne Boleyn's coronation.

Gentlemen, two, in *Measure for Measure*, who engage in bawdy talk with Lucio about sex and venereal disease. All very much Shakespeare, and contemporary; cf. my *Simon Forman: Sex and Society in Shakespeare's Age*.

Gentlemen, four of them, bring news to Montano, former governor of Cyprus, of the Turkish fleet and welcome Desdemona, Cassio, Iago and their train from Venice to the aid of Cyprus. *Othello*.

Gentlewoman in *Macbeth*, attendant on Lady Macbeth, reports on her sleep-walking, with the sinister line:

> *Heaven knows what she has known.*

George, duke of Clarence. *See* Clarence.

Gertrude, Queen of Denmark, Hamlet's mother, his father's wife. Claudius, not content with murdering his brother to take his throne, takes also his wife. Hence the tragedy: *Hamlet* is the greatest of all in the Elizabethan genre of revenge plays.

It was not nice of the Queen to marry the brother so soon after her husband's death - 'the funeral baked meats did coldly furnish forth the marriage tables'. But she is a not very intelligent woman, caught in the web of circumstance she does not understand. When Hamlet speaks to the Ghost of his father, whom she cannot see though in her presence, she very naturally concludes, 'Alas, he's mad.'

She cannot understand her brilliant, tormented son, though he does succeed in bringing home to her, in a wonderful scene alone with her, her guilt in marrying the brother-in-law, again not understanding that he was the murderer.

She is all woman, with kind impulses, sympathetic to Ophelia in her trouble and wishing that she might have married her son and all been happy.

> *I hoped thou shouldst have been my*
>   *Hamlet's wife.*
> *I thought thy bride-bed to have decked,*
>   *sweet maid,*
> *And not have strewed thy grave.*

In truth, she is a not unsympathetic - but rather pathetic - character, victim too in a world of passion and grief. And should be performed as such. Gertrude dotes on Hamlet - Claudius says that she 'lives almost by his looks'. Which makes his reproaches to her, holding up the glass to her character all the more wounding - to the spectator heart-rending. *Hamlet*.

Ghost of the dead King. *Hamlet*. This is Hamlet's dead father, who appears to him to lay upon him the injunction to revenge his murder. This sets going the action.

Ghosts, many appear in the Plays, cf. Anne, Banquo, Buckingham, Julius Caesar, Clarence, Edward, Hastings, Henry VI, Rivers, Vaughan, York.

Glamis, Thane of. *See* Macbeth.

Glansdale, Sir William. *1 Henry VI*.

Glendower, Owen, d. *c.* 1416, famous leader of Welsh resistance to Henry IV. Treated unjustly, he raised North Wales against the English and even extended his power into South Wales. He allied himself with Mortimer, to whom he married his daughter, and with the Percies in rebellion. He makes a brief appearance in *Richard II*, but is an important character in *1 Henry IV*. He had the charisma which Shakespeare gives him; no one knows when he died or where he was buried.

Gloucester, earl of, in *King Lear* is loyal to the King and for this is blinded by Cornwall and Regan. He has his own tragedy in that his mind is poisoned against his son Edgar, by his bastard son Edmund. An old man leads Gloucester towards Dover, his true son Edgar encountering him on the way and frustrating him in his design of throwing himself from the cliff, so famously described.

Shakespeare's Company played at Dover in the summer of 1606; the play was written that summer and autumn. So Shakespeare's Cliff there is properly named.

Gloucester, duchess of, in *Richard II*: Eleanor Bohun, wife of Thomas of Woodstock, duke, youngest son of Edward III, uncle of Richard.

Gloucester, Humphry, duke of, and wife. *See* Humphry.

Gloucester, Richard, duke of. *See* Richard III.

Gobbo, father of Lancelot. *The Merchant of Venice*.

Gobbo, Lancelot, servant to Shylock. *The Merchant of Venice*. His realistic below-stairs language gives comic relief.

Goffe, Matthew, opponent of Jack Cade. *2 Henry VI*.

Goneril, eldest of King Lear's daughters, married to the Duke of Albany, whom she despises for his kindly, but ineffectual, feeling towards her father. She is really in love with Gloucester's bastard son, Edmund. But so is her sister Regan - hence deadly rivalry between them. In the end Goneril poisons her sister, and kills herself. It has sometimes been discussed which of these monsters is worse. Lear supposes Goneril, for she is more open and first to display ingratitude and a cruel temper. There is little to choose between them, though Goneril does kill her sister. *King Lear*.

Gonzago, duke and wife, parts assumed by the Players in *Hamlet*.

Gonzalo, an old councillor in *The Tempest*, whom Shakespeare uses to refute Montaigne's idealistic picture of primitive communism.

> *In the commonwealth . . .*
> *no kind of traffic*
> *Would I admit. No name of magistrate.*
> *Letters should not be known. Riches,*
> *poverty,*
> *And use of service, none. Contract,*
> *succession,*
> *Bourn, bound of land, tilth, vineyard, none . . .*
> *No occupation, all men idle, all,*
> *And women too, but innocent and pure.*

Someone inquires:

> *No marrying among his subjects?*

Another replies:

> *None, man: all idle - whores and knaves.*

William Shakespeare's common sense told him what nonsense this was; and from his own experience in Warwickshire, where peasants were removing bounds and rioting against enclosures at this time. In the play a conspiracy is concocted - instigated by the primitive innocent, Caliban.

Gower, captain in Henry V's army. *Henry V.*

Gower, supporter of the King. *2 Henry IV.*

Gower, John, 14th-century poet, is called up from the past to act as Chorus, in antique verse, in *Pericles*. The story mainly came from his *Confessio Amantis*. We should remember that his monument was a dominant feature of the great church neighbouring the Globe Theatre, then St Saviour's, now Southwark cathedral.

Grandpré, French lord. *Henry V.*

Gratiano, Brabantio's brother, uncle of Desdemona. *Othello*.

Gratiano, friend of Antonio the Merchant. *The Merchant of Venice*.

Gravediggers in *Hamlet*, surely the most memorable in literature. The gravedigger and the sexton, digging Ophelia's grave, are realistic caricatures drawn from Shakespeare's familiar observation of such types, compare his constables and headboroughs, gaolers and pimps. Their talk offers some very pertinent comments on the high life going on above them, the lawyers and politicians, and again one in Shakespeare's own profession, a famous actor who had made the Court laugh in his time - Yorick (Tarleton?).

Their remarkable scene with Hamlet and Horatio among the graves adds point to Dr Johnson's praise of the play for its *variety* against all his classical predilections. 'The scenes are interchangeably diversified with merriment and solemnity; with merriment that includes judicious and instructive observations, and solemnity not strained by poetical violence above the natural sentiments of man.'

In short, *Hamlet* - like Beethoven's 'Eroica' - has *everything*.

Green, Sir Henry, d. 1399. One of Richard II's agents, captured and executed at Bristol. *Richard II.*

Gregory (a) a Capulet follower, talks realistic bawdy with another in a Verona street, both armed and ready to quarrel with a Montague man. *Romeo and Juliet*. (b) A servant in *The Taming of the Shrew*.

Gremio, suitor to Bianca. *The Taming of the Shrew*.

Grey, Lord Richard, *Richard III*.

Grey, Sir Thomas, *Henry V*.

Griffith, gentleman usher to Queen Katharine. *Henry VIII*.

Groom, Richard II's. *Richard II*.

Grumio, servant to Petruchio. *The Taming of the Shrew*.

Guards, two Volscian. *Coriolanus*.

Guardsmen, First and Second, in *Antony and Cleopatra*.

Guiderius, son of Cymbeline, supposed lost but brought up in Wales under the disguised name of Polydore, by the banished courtier Belarius. *Cymbeline*.

Guildenstern, a former companion, with Rosencrantz, of Hamlet, whom King Claudius has sent for to spy on him. In a brilliant showdown Hamlet forces these false friends to confess that they were sent for. Later Claudius sends them with him to England, with a secret order for his execution. On the ship Hamlet substitutes a commission for theirs:

> 'Tis dangerous when the baser nature comes
> Between the pass and fell incensèd points
> Of mighty opposites.   Hamlet.

Guildford, Sir Henry, 1489-1532, Master of the Horse, Comptroller of the Household. *Henry VIII*.

Gurney, James, servant of Lady Faulconbridge. *King John*.

Haberdasher, a, appears in *The Taming of the Shrew*.

Hal, Prince. *See* Henry V.

Hamlet, subject of Shakespeare's greatest play, called after him. Son of the murdered king, whose Ghost appears to him to lay upon him the duty of revenging his death. Shakespeare has put something of himself into this character: for one thing his sheer intellectual brilliance; for another, one has a singular impression of inwardness. More than intimacy - a soul is exposed.

His father's murder is the springboard of the play, and the question of the succession to the throne is in the background. Hamlet's uncle, the murderer, stands between Hamlet's election and his hopes. He needs external corroboration of his uncle's guilt - hence his putting on the inset play and Claudius's startled recognition of the fact. Why does not Hamlet kill him at once? Because he catches his uncle at prayer, repenting his crime to God, his repentant soul would go to heaven. Events would be deprived of their unfolding, the play cut short, aborted.

As it is, we are shown Hamlet in every relationship, as with no other character in the plays: in relation to his father, to his mother and his uncle, his friends and enemies, to Ophelia whom he loves and her father whom he baits brilliantly and kills accidentally. Hamlet's verbal torturing of Ophelia and himself is heartbreaking, yet convincing psychologically - because he thinks their love is betrayed.

We are even given Hamlet as producer of a play, with his views on acting - clearly Shakespeare's own, unquestionably autobiographical.

At the end of all, the Prince of Norway commands:

> *Bear Hamlet like a soldier to the stage,*
> *For he was likely, had he been put on,*
> *To have proved most royal.*

Hamlet was yet young. Is there in the whole of literature, a character more rich and complex, yet simple and moving?

Harcourt, supporter of the King. *2 Henry IV.*

Harfleur, governor of. *Henry V.*

Hastings, lord, opponent of the King. *2 Henry IV.* Actually he was Sir Edward Hastings, 1381-1437, claimant of the barony.

Hastings, William, lord, *c.* 1430-1483. Devoted Yorkist, bosom friend of Edward IV. Refusing to go along with Richard's design to usurp his nephew's throne, he was summarily beheaded - the signal for Richard's *coup d'état. 3 Henry VI, Richard III.*

Hastings' Messenger. *Richard III.*

Headborough, *see* Verges.

Hecate, goddess of the underworld, an addition by Middleton to Shakespeare's play. *Macbeth.*

Hector (a) Trojan hero, Priam's son. *Troilus and Cressida.*
(b) Impersonated by Armado, *Love's Labour's Lost.*

Helen, most beautiful of women in Greek legend, wife of Menelaus, carried off by Paris to Troy, thus starting the foolish Trojan war. *Troilus and Cressida.*

Helen, a lady attending on Imogen. *Cymbeline.*

Helena, a doctor's daughter, waiting on the Countess of Rousillon, in love with her son, Count Bertram. *All's Well That Ends Well.*

Helena, in love with Demetrius. *A Midsummer Night's Dream.*

Helenus, one of King Priam's too many sons. *Troilus and Cressida.*

Helicanus, an ancient lord of Tyre, faithful to Pericles. *Pericles.*

Henry III, 1207-1272, son of King John, has a small part at the end of *King John*. Builder of Westminster Abbey.

Henry IV, 1367-1413, eldest son of John of Gaunt. Born at Bolingbroke (Lincolnshire), by which name he was popularly known. An able soldier, he went on 'crusade' with the Teutonic Knights of Prussia, and then made the pilgrimage across Europe to Venice, for Jerusalem. Exiled by Richard II, who seized his inheritance on Gaunt's death, Henry returned to claim it, but was propelled to the throne, for his own self-preservation, and called to it by the will of Church and State expressed in Parliament. Both Henry and Gaunt attached importance to the fact that they were next in the male line to the succession.

Henry proved an able king, but his possession of the Crown was challenged by his former allies, the Percies, whom he defeated at Shrewsbury, 1403; and again some years later.

With the King's failing health, there developed a contest for power, and a pathetic father-son complex. It is now known, what the Victorians did not know, that Shakespeare was in keeping with the tradition about the madcap side to Prince Henry's youth. The King suffered from a succession of strokes, and died in Jerusalem Chamber at Westminster Abbey, but lies buried at Canterbury.

Henry's reign was filled with trouble and continued opposition, from his deposition of Richard II, necessary as that was. From that came the split within the royal house between Lancaster and York, and hence the Wars of the Roses.

Shakespeare gives us a sympathetic portrait of the King, many aspects authentic historically: his popularity as Bolingbroke, depicted in *Richard II*, the strains upon him as king, and the pathos of his relationship with his son, in *1* and *2 Henry IV*.

Henry V, 1387-1422, eldest son of Henry IV. Born at Monmouth, he spent much of his youth fighting as a soldier, and emerged a seasoned commander. On his accession to the throne he underwent a religious conversion. Secure in the succession, he decided to revive Edward III's claim (in the female line) to the French throne. At Agincourt in 1415 Henry won a famous victory against immensely superior forces. France was divided between the party of the Dauphin and that of the Duke of Burgundy.

By the treaty of Troyes, 1420, Henry was declared heir to Charles VI, meanwhile to govern in his name, and married his daughter Katharine. Struck by fatal disease, he died at Vincennes in 1422 aged thirty-five.

Henry V was not only a military commander of exceptional ability but the ablest of English medieval kings, with a great aptitude for government and zeal for justice. To the Elizabethans he was a hero-king, and

Henry V has a certain epic quality. Shakespeare goes beneath the surface in portraying Prince Hal with his youthful pranks in *Henry IV*, as well as the sovereign confronting his responsibilities before God on the eve of Agincourt. As for the gallant soldier's courtship of the French princess - charming, of course; but with Henry V all was politics, as was his duty: '*un être politique*', as Napoleon described himself.

Henry VI, 1421-1471, son of Henry V and Katharine of France, born at Windsor. Only a year old at his father's death, there followed a long minority during which the Council ruled. But it was divided between the popular war-party, headed by his uncle, Humphry, duke of Gloucester; and his great-uncle, Cardinal Beaufort, who favoured peace. Under the latter's influence Suffolk negotiated a truce and a marriage on unfavourable terms with Margaret of Anjou. Maine was surrendered, Guienne lost, and eventually Normandy itself.

Failure all round produced internal unrest and precipitated the attempt of Richard, duke of York, to gain power. Popular unrest resulted in Jack Cade's Rising. In 1453 Henry suffered a complete breakdown. During this interval his son Edward, Prince of Wales, was born. On Henry's recovery York was excluded from power, and open conflict between Yorkists and Lancastrians ensued.

Another breakdown for the King was followed by his attempt at a compromise, recognising York as heir to the throne. Margaret would not accept this, nor would Parliament recognise York's attempt to occupy the throne, and he was killed at the battle of Wakefield. His much abler son, Edward, reversed the issue by his military ability and victory at Towton. Henry escaped to Scotland, then wandered about the North Country in disguise until captured and incarcerated in the Tower.

In 1470-1, Edward IV having temporarily lost the

throne, Henry VI was restored. This did not last. Edward returned to defeat Warwick at Barnet, and Henry's son was killed at Tewkesbury. A clean sweep of the Lancastrian royal house could now be made, and Henry was murdered in the Tower.

This would not have happened if he had been competent as a ruler. Exceptionally pious, he should have been a churchman; he could not bear the ulcerated feuds of politics and infinitely preferred a simple life - Shakespeare caught this well. Henry did his duty as a patron of learning and of universities, and his memory is kept green by his great foundations of Eton and King's College, Cambridge.

So long and confused a reign, with its hapless minority, presented a problem for the commencing dramatist. He had to take liberties with Henry's age, but attributes of his character are authentically presented: his gentleness and simplicity, his humanity and hatred of carnage, his distaste for the burdens of kingship and his incapacity for them - which led to tragedy for himself and for the country.

Henry VII, *see* Richmond.

Henry VIII, 1491-1547, son of Henry VII and Elizabeth of York. On Prince Arthur's death he succeeded him as heir and also to his wife, Katharine of Aragon, by which match came many troubles later. Henry inherited his Yorkist grandfather, Edward IV's marked characteristics: his girth, fondness for outdoor activities and sport, political ability, *bonhommie*, along with a vein of capricious cruelty. Unlike his Tudor father he was extravagant and exhibitionist, letting the country in for three French wars which exhausted the Crown's resources.

He used Cardinal Wolsey's immense ability to win prestige in Europe. With no male heir, he sought a divorce from Katharine as his brother's former wife: impossible to obtain from the Pope, who was in the hands of her nephew, the Emperor Charles V. Falling passionately in love with Anne Boleyn, when she became pregnant, he secretly married her in the hope of a son. She produced a daughter, Elizabeth I. Three years later he had Anne executed on trumped-up charges.

We need not follow Henry's subsequent matrimonial misadventures, since Shakespeare does not deal with them but contents himself with selected aspects of the reign: the fall of Buckingham, then of Wolsey, to the death of Katharine, ending with the baptism of Princess Elizabeth.

It was not possible to tell the whole truth about Henry VIII, even in the reign of James I, and Shakespeare's portrait of him is a mere torso, conserving - tactfully as usual - Henry's royal dignity, formal courtesy and overwhelming presence, with his idiosyncratic and rather sinister 'Ha!' *Henry VIII.*

Herald, Othello's in the play reads his proclamation of victory over the Turkish fleet.

Heralds, *Coriolanus, King Lear, 1 and 2 Henry VI, King John, Richard II. See also* Montjoy.

Herbert, Sir Walter. Yorkist, but joined Richmond in Wales on his way to Bosworth. *Richard III.*

Hercules, impersonated by Moth. *Love's Labour's Lost.*

Hereford, duke of, i.e. Bolingbroke. *See* Henry IV.

Hermia, daughter of Egeus, in love with Lysander. *A Midsummer Night's Dream.*

Hermione, queen to Leontes, unjustly put away by him. *The Winter's Tale.*

Herne the Hunter, impersonated by Falstaff. *The Merry Wives of Windsor.*

Hero, daughter of Leonato, victim of a frame-up by the villainous Don John. *Much Ado About Nothing.*

Hippolyta, Queen of the Amazons, betrothed to Theseus, duke of Athens. *A Midsummer Night's Dream.*

Holland, John, one of Cade's rebels. *2 Henry VI. See also* Exeter, Surrey.

Holofernes, a schoolmaster. *Love's Labour's Lost* (a touch of caricature of Florio, Southampton's tutor, in him).

Horatio, Hamlet's faithful friend, on whom alone he can rely in the treachery and suspicion of the Court. He too sees the Ghost of Hamlet's father, and swears to keep the secret, being the recipient of the famous lines:

> *There are more things in heaven and earth, Horatio,*
> *Than are dreamt of in your philosophy.*

And at the end of all it falls to him to pronounce his farewell:

> *Now cracks a noble heart. Good night, sweet Prince,*
> *And flights of angels sing thee to thy rest.*
> *Hamlet.*

Horner, Thomas, armourer, with his man. *2 Henry VI.*

Hortensio, suitor to Bianca. *The Taming of the Shrew.*

Hortensius, servant of one of Timon's creditors. *Timon of Athens.*

Host, of the Garter inn at Windsor. *The Merry Wives of Windsor*.

Host, of an inn in Milan. *The Two Gentlemen of Verona*.

Hostess, of an ale-house on the heath. Induction to *The Taming of the Shrew*.

Hostess, of tavern in East Cheap. *Henry V. And see* Mistress Quickly.

Hostilius, a stranger. *Timon of Athens*.

Hotspur, *see* Henry Percy.

Howard, *see* Norfolk, Surrey.

Hubert de Burgh, d. 1243, chamberlain to King John. Probably had custody of John's nephew, Arthur, in Normandy for a time. *King John*.

Hume, John, a priest. *2 Henry VI*.

Humphry, duke of Gloucester, 1391-1447, youngest son of Henry IV. Named Protector of his nephew, the infant Henry VI, he quarrelled for years with his uncle, Cardinal Beaufort, who favoured a peace policy. Humphry, advocate of a war policy, was always popular: 'the good Duke Humphry'. He appears in *2 Henry IV, Henry V*, but most fully in *1* and *2 Henry VI*. His second duchess, Eleanor Cobham, had been his mistress. Accused of witchcraft in the hope of making her husband king, she was made to do penance, imprisoned and exiled from Court. Evidently a liability to poor Humphry. The affair makes effective scenes in *2 Henry VI*.

Huntingdon, earl of, John Holland, 1395-1447. *Henry V*.

Huntsmen. The Induction to *The Taming of the Shrew*.

Hymen, god of married love, appears to marry up the lovers at the end of *As You Like It*.

Iachimo, in *Cymbeline*, a light-hearted and light-headed villain, rather than a deep-dyed villain like Iago, who makes a wager with Leonatus in exile as to the chastity of his wife, Imogen. He penetrates her bedroom, though not herself, unlike Tarquin with Lucrece - a situation Shakespeare was recalling.

Iago, the villain of *Othello*, is the most interesting character in the play, and one of the most powerful in all Shakespeare. He is an incarnation of evil, with no redeeming feature - except perhaps his intellectuality, the sheer skill with which he can fascinate his victims, all of them and of varying kinds. His is a triumph of will, of malignant will, over virtue and innocence, credulity and stupidity.

'Virtue? A fig. 'Tis in ourselves that we are thus, or thus. Our bodies are our gardens, to the which our wills are gardeners.'

It is often held that Iago is an exemplar of 'motiveless malignity'. This is not so: it is twice suggested that he suspects the sexy Moor with his wife; and Othello has preferred Cassio, a Florentine, to be his Lieutenant, in spite of Iago's superior claims from experience and the backing of 'three great ones of the city in personal suit'. And he is Othello's ancient, or ensign:

> *I know my price, I am worth no worse a*
> *place.*

So he hates the Moor, and is determined on revenge. The

skill with which he pursues it is masterly; one cannot but admire it - it forfeits sympathy when people are such fools as to fall for it.

Iago knows - as Hitler well knew - that the obvious way to take people in is to tell them the truth. So he actually warns Othello against jealousy:

> O beware, my lord, of jealousy:
> It is the green-eyed monster which doth mock
> The meat it feeds on.

He appears to defend Cassio, whom he is bent on ruining in Othello's opinion - so Othello is fool enough to be all the more convinced of Iago's honesty. 'Honest Iago', indeed, as he thinks to the very end.

It has not been appreciated that Iago could find it in mind - if not in heart - even to love his victim (such psychological twists are diagnosed today: Shakespeare intuited them):

> Now I do love her too,
> Not out of absolute lust, though peradventure
> I stand accountant for as great a sin.

At the beginning he warns, 'I am not what I am'; and at the very end,

> Demand me nothing. What you know you
> know.
> From this time forth, I never will speak
> word.

He will carry the secret of himself to the grave; but, a complex character, most rewarding to study, in the course of his trajectory he reveals a world of foolery. He must have been motivated too by contempt for humans (as was Hitler).

Iden, Alexander, Kentish gentleman, kills Jack Cade in his garden. *2 Henry VI.*

Illyria, duke of. *See* Orsino.

Imogen, Cymbeline's daughter by a former wife, rejects the suit of her step-mother's son and marries beneath her - for she appears as the heiress to the kingdom - a gentleman, Leonatus Posthumus. He has to fly the realm, and in Rome makes a wager with a scheming Italian to try the virtue of his wife at home. Iachimo enters her bedroom in a trunk, and is able to describe not only her room but her physical attributes - a mole, etc - recognisably and authentically. Leonatus is taken in, and seeks revenge: hence the play's sub-plot.

Imogen is of the race of Shakespeare's pure, innocent, ideal young women, like Miranda, Perdita, or Desdemona. She too goes through her trial - the circumstances of which repeat something from *The Rape of Lucrece*. But it does not end tragically; in *Cymbeline* as in the last romance-plays, all ends happily.

Iras, attendant on Cleopatra, who brings her robe and crown to array her for death; to whom she addresses the famous lines,

> *Give me my robe, put on my crown, I have*
> *Immortal longings in me.*

Iris, goddess presented by a spirit in the masque. *The Tempest.*

Isabel, Richard II's second queen, 1389-1409, daughter of Charles VI of France, married to Richard at the age of seven in pledge of peace. Shakespeare makes her a mature woman for dramatic reasons. *Richard II.*

Isabel (Isabeau of Bavaria), wife of Charles VI of France, 1371-1435. With a demented husband, she was no better than she should be. Rejecting her son the Dauphin, as not her husband's, she went over to Henry V and supported his marriage to her daughter Katharine. *Henry V.*

Isabella, the errant Claudio's too virtuous sister, who refuses to yield her virtue to the Duke's Deputy, even to save her brother's life. This inhumanity, however, gives her a powerful part. *Measure for Measure.*

Jamy, Scottish captain in Henry V's army, whose lingo Shakespeare takes off. *Henry V*.

Jaquenetta, a country wench. *Love's Labour's Lost*.

Jaques, melancholy cynic, attending on Duke Senior. *As You Like It*.

Jaques de Boys, a brother of Orlando. *As You Like It*.

Jessica, Shylock's daughter, who absconds from her father for love of Lorenzo. This is supposed to be comic, and was to the Elizabethans. But, today, do we wholly sympathise with her? *The Merchant of Venice*.

Jeweller, to Timon. *Timon of Athens*.

Joan of Arc (or Joan Pucelle), 1412-1431. Heroine of the French resistance to the English, revived French morale by raising the siege of Orléans, defeating the English at Patay, and leading Charles VII to coronation at Rheims. Captured by the Burgundians, she was sold to the English, condemned as a witch and burnt at Rouen. Today recognised as a saint. Shakespeare's attitude towards her in his earliest work is ambivalent, since credulous medievals - even the bishop of Beauvais - regarded her as a witch, and so too do Shakespeare's authorities. Some humanity, however, comes breaking through, as in the mature Shakespeare with Shylock. Her father, an old shepherd, also appears. *1 Henry VI*.

John, King, *c.* 1167-1216, youngest son of Henry II, and brother of Richard Coeur-de-lion. He inherited the passionate impulsiveness of his Angevin family, together with its mercurial changeability. On Richard's death in 1199 John was acknowledged king, and married Isabella of Angoulême. Involved in continual war to defend his inheritance of Normandy, Anjou, etc, against the designs of the able French king Philip, John captured Arthur of Brittany.

Losing Normandy, he encountered opposition from the Anglo-Norman barons in England, and entered upon a prolonged conflict with the Church. Though the Pope had conferred upon him the lordship of Ireland, John was now excommunicated and England laid under interdict. There ensued civil war, and at Runnymede near Windsor John was forced to agree to Magna Carta to rule by custom and law, and to respect the liberties of the Church.

This gave him a party to resist the invasion of the French under Philip's son, Louis the Dauphin, and regained the support of the Pope who sent the legate Pandulph to negotiate peace. In the midst of the crisis John died, and was buried in his favourite Worcester cathedral.

Shakespeare makes some use of the patriotic appeal, popular in his time, against Papal claims, but without the Protestant rant of others, like John Bale. Again Shakespeare tactfully gives a more favourable picture of the King than historical facts warrant. *King John.*

John, Prince, 1389-1435, 3rd son of Henry IV. *1* and *2 Henry IV*, where he smartly turns the tables on rebel Archbishop Scrope. In *1 Henry VI* he appears as Duke of Bedford, when he ruled as Regent in France for his nephew, Henry VI. A man of ability and patron of the arts, he died and was buried at Rouen.

See also Don John, Friar John.

John Rugby, servant to Doctor Caius. *The Merry Wives of Windsor.*

Joseph, *The Taming of the Shrew.*

Jourdain, Margery, a witch. *2 Henry VI.*

Judas Maccabeus, impersonated by Holofernes, *Love's Labour's Lost.*

Julia, a lady of Verona, in *The Two Gentlemen of Verona.* Proteus is at first in love with her, but deserts her for his friend Valentine's girl, Silvia.

Juliet, betrothed to and pregnant by Claudio, the situation which provides the issue in *Measure for Measure.*

Juliet, daughter of Capulet, head of that house at feud with the Montagues in Verona. But she and Romeo fall passionately in love - fatally, for he is Montague's son. Juliet is sought in love by Count Paris, 'the County Paris', whom her parents urge upon her as a suitable marriage. Hence the intrigue upon which the action turns: how is she to get out of it, when she is secretly married to Romeo?

Her passion for him is as great as his for her - they are both young, when the desire for sex is apt to be insatiable. The play gives the strongest impression of that - far more than *Antony and Cleopatra* with which it has been compared, for by then Shakespeare was older, and disillusioned.

It is Juliet, not Romeo - properly enough, so true to human nature - who has forebodings of too intense a love, such insatiable enjoyment of each other:

> *O God, I have an ill-divining soul.*
> *Methinks I see thee now thou art so low*
> *As one dead in the bottom of a tomb.*

And so it turned out. *Romeo and Juliet.*

Juliet, betrothed to and pregnant by Claudio, the situation which sets going the play. *Measure for Measure.*

Julius Caesar, *see* Caesar.

Junius Brutus, tribune of the people and naturally a demagogue, who incites the mob against the hero. *Coriolanus.*

Jupiter, appears in the masque in *Cymbeline*, leaving an oracle portending the prosperity of the King and his family.

Justice, Lord Chief. *2 Henry IV.* This was Sir William Gascoigne, *c.* 1350-1419. His servant also appears.

Katharine of Aragon, Henry VIII's queen, 1485-1536. First married to Henry's brother, Prince Arthur, who died young - hence the trouble later. Her subsequent marriage to Henry required a papal dispensation, and there were doubts about its validity from the first. These were confirmed in Henry's mind when she failed to produce a male heir and he fell in love with Anne Boleyn. *Henry VIII.*

Katharine, Henry V's queen, 1401-1437, daughter of Charles VI of France. Married to Henry at Troyes 1420, crowned at Westminster 1421; her son Henry VI born 2 December 1421. After Henry V's death she secretly married Owen Tudor, one of his following; their son, Edmund earl of Richmond, married Margaret Beaufort, eventual heiress-general of John of Gaunt and of the Lancastrian claim to the throne, which she transmitted to her son, Henry VII. *Henry V.* The scenes in French were probably written when Shakespeare lodged with the French Montjoy family in Silver Street.

Katharine, lady attendant on the Princess of France in *Love's Labour's Lost.*

Katharine, or Kate, daughter to Baptista in *The Taming of the Shrew.* She is the shrew, ill-tempered and intolerable, who is cured and finally subjugated by Petruchio's combination of firmness and love. She emerges from her ordeal as the ideal Elizabethan wife, submissive and obedient to husband. Modern people find this consummation difficult to understand - *nous avons changé tout cela* - and are apt to misinterpret it. It should be seen in contemporary terms: Shakespeare's wife appears to have made no trouble, whatever she had to put up with.

Keeper, Clarence's, in the Tower. *Richard III*.

Keeper, of Richard II. *Richard II*.

Keepers, two park-, who capture Henry VI wandering in the North. *3 Henry VI*.

Kent, earl of, in *King Lear* is the faithful follower of the King, who sends him as messenger to Regan and her husband. They put him in the stocks, a punishment reserved for offenders of base condition: thus a grievous insult to an earl, still more to the messenger of the King, her father - which enrages him still further. Gloucester, who is old Kent's 'honoured friend', protests. Kent follows the King faithfully through the wilds and tempest to his destined end. When Albany would put the rule of the realm upon him, his last words are:

> *I have a journey, sir, shortly to go.*
> *My master calls me. I must not say no.*

Labeo, follower of Brutus. *Julius Caesar.*

Laertes, Polonius's son, Ophelia's brother in *Hamlet*. When he returns from abroad he has *his* father's death, his sister driven desperate, to avenge on Hamlet. He is a swordsman, and the King easily works upon him by arousing his envy of Hamlet's fencing ability. The King lays a wager to excite a bout between them and cheats by choosing a sword unbated. Laertes makes sure by anointing the point with venom; the King doubly sure by poisoning Hamlet's drink.

Lafeu, a wise old lord who puts Parolles down. *All's Well That Ends Well.*

Lancaster, *see* Gaunt, Prince John.

Lartius, Titus. *Coriolanus.*

Launce, servant to Proteus in *The Two Gentlemen of Verona*. A direct and realistic portrayal of an Elizabethan manservant, with only a slight element of caricature, he is the most attractive figure in the play. His dog also is given a character.

Lavache, jester to the countess of Rousillon. *All's Well That Ends Well.*

Lavinia, Titus's daughter, is raped and mutilated in *Titus*

Andronicus after the story of Tereus and Philomel in Ovid, Shakespeare's favourite classical poet, himself coming to the theatre from teaching, in a country school according to John Aubrey.

Lawyer, a. *1 Henry VI.*

Lear, king of Britain, who in the play *King Lear*, written in 1606, brings all his troubles upon himself by divesting himself of his rule, and dividing his kingdom between his two daughters, Goneril and Regan, rejecting his youngest daughter Cordelia. The treatment he receives at the hands of the first two drives him mad. His tragic experience is a revelation as to the truth of life: hitherto he has lived in a fantasy world, his head turned by kingship, obeisance and everybody hanging on his word. The play portrays his progressive education in reality through suffering.

His daughters may be supposed to know him best. Regan: 'he hath ever but slenderly known himself'. Goneril: 'The best and soundest of his time hath been but rash...' His rashness and impetuosity - and then expecting to be treated as a king as before, and with the kindness due to an ageing father who has been too generous - lead to his undoing.

Madness - real in Lear's case, affected in Hamlet's - was most effective on the stage, as other plays of the time testify, notably Kyd's *The Spanish Tragedy*. *Hamlet* and *King Lear* are the twin peaks' of Shakespeare's achievement in tragedy. They offer a rewarding contrast: both are inner dramas of a soul in torment, but Hamlet's comes about through no fault of his own, Lear's is self-induced through his own folly. This gives us the less sympathy with an old man who might have learned from a lifetime, as against a young man caught in a web of fatal circumstance. Lear's fate is, however, given an almost epic dimension by its extrapolation into the outer world of storm and tempest, mirroring the inner tragedies of men's souls, those of others than King Lear portrayed in accordance with their varying characters and experience.

Le Beau, courtier attending on Duke Frederick. *As You Like It.*

Le Fer, Monsieur. *Henry V.*

Legate, a. *1 Henry VI.*

Lena, *see* **Popilius**.

Lennox, Scottish noble, knocks loudly at the gate of Macbeth's castle for admittance the night of King Duncan's murder; expresses suspicion of the events that followed. *Macbeth.*

Leonardo, servant to Bassanio. *The Merchant of Venice.*

Leonato, *Much Ado About Nothing.*

Leonatus, *see* **Posthumus, Sicilius**.

Leonine, servant to Dionyza, was to have murdered Marina at her command. *Pericles.*

Leontes, king of Sicilia, is psychotically jealous of his old friend Polixenes' friendship with his wife, Hermione, whom he condemns to trial. She is thought to die in giving birth to a daughter, whom he consigns to oblivion. His little son dies. A whole train of consequences is set in motion by his quasi-madness. It is an astonishing portrayal of psychosis, in which Shakespeare has intuited the findings of modern psychology, and just how it works, suspicion confirmed by every trifle, etc. *The Winter's Tale.*

Lepidus, M. Aemelius, d. 13 BC. One of the Triumvirs who, after Caesar's death, headed his party with Octavius and Antony. *Julius Caesar* and *Antony and Cleopatra*.

Lewis the Dauphin, *see* Louis VIII.

Lewis the Dauphin, in *Henry V*, died shortly after Agincourt, 1415.

Licio, name assumed by Hortensio.

Lieutenant to Aufidius. *Coriolanus*.

Lieutenants of the Tower, 2 and *3 Henry VI, Richard III, Sir Thomas More*.

Ligarius, Q., a conspirator against Caesar, in spite of being pardoned by him for fighting against him. *Julius Caesar*. After Caesar's death Ligarius and his two brothers perished in the proscription by the Triumvirs.

Lincoln, bishop of. *Henry VIII*. This was John Longland, 1473-1547.

Lincoln, John, a broker. *Sir Thomas More*.

Lodovico, kinsman of Brabantio. *Othello*.

London, bishop of, John Stokesley, *c.* 1475-1539. *Henry VIII*.

London, Lord Mayor of (a) *1 Henry VI*. (b) *Henry VIII*. (c) *Richard III*. (d) *Sir Thomas More*.

Longaville (Longueville), French lord attendant on Navarre. *Love's Labour's Lost*.

Lord, a, unnamed, in the Induction to *The Taming of the Shrew*, who plays the trick on the drunken tinker, Christopher Sly, of inducing him to believe that he is himself a lord, with attendants, equipment, etc.

Lords, First and Second. *All's Well That Ends Well.*

Lords, two, of Cymbeline's Court. *Cymbeline.*

Lorenzo, the Christian in love with Jessica who steals her from her father, Shylock. *The Merchant of Venice.*

Louis VIII, of France, 1187-1226. As Dauphin he invaded England in alliance with King John's barons, but was defeated and withdrew. *King John.*

Louis XI, of France, 1423-1483, encouraged Warwick 'the kingmaker' and Queen Margaret to invade England - hence the fatal fields of Barnet and Tewkesbury. *3 Henry VI.*

Lovell, lord, named Sir Thomas, in *Richard III*, was actually Francis, a Yorkist who disappeared after the battle of Stoke, 1487.

Lovell, Sir Thomas. *Henry VIII.* He fought for Henry VII at Bosworth, d. 1524.

Luce, servant to Adriana. *The Comedy of Errors.*

Lucentio, in love with the agreeable Bianca. *The Taming of the Shrew.*

Lucetta, waiting woman to Julia. *The Two Gentlemen of Verona.*

Luciana, sister of Adriana. *The Comedy of Errors.*

Lucianus, part assumed by a player. *Hamlet.*

Lucilius (a) friend of Brutus and Cassius. *Julius Caesar.* (b) Servant of Timon. *Timon of Athens.*

Lucio - the choice of name is suggestive - a licentious and free-spoken young gentleman in *Measure for Measure.* Described as a 'fantastic', he is an engaging rascal, with no morals and no inhibitions, and provides comic relief in this rather sombre play. One of those who like to think that they are in the know and retail gossip about public figures, he scandalises the absent Duke. For this he gets his come-uppance from the Duke returned, who condemns him to marry a whore: 'Marrying a punk, my lord, is pressing to death, whipping, and hanging.'

Lucius (a) Caius, *Cymbeline.* (b) Brutus's slave boy. *Julius Caesar.* (c) One of Timon's false friends. *Timon of Athens.* (d) Son of Titus. *Titus Andronicus.*

Lucullus, one of Timon's mean friends. *Timon of Athens.*

Lucy, Sir William. *1 Henry VI.* His descendants were the leading family in Shakespeare's day at Stratford.

Lychorida, nurse to Marina. *Pericles.*

Lymoges, *see* Austria.

Lysander, in love with Hermia. *A Midsummer Night's Dream.*

Lysimachus, governor of Mytilene, visits the brothel in disguise where Marina is confined, and is converted from his fell intent by her virtuous conversation. *Pericles.*

Macbeth, hero – for there is something heroic about him, for all that he is a murderer – of the play of his name. To him appear the Three Witches, who foretell that he will become Thane of Cawdor and then King. But are these apparitions extrapolations of his subconscious wishes? We see again how much Shakespeare is in keeping with the findings of modern psychology: he is indeed, as Ben Jonson said, 'for all time'.

But Banquo had seen these apparitions too, and their prophecy is corroborated when King Duncan makes Macbeth, already Thane of Glamis, Thane of Cawdor. The ambition to become king is irresistible. But when he hesitates to kill the King it is his relentless wife who steels his purpose, in phrases that have become commonplaces in the language:

> *Letting I dare not wait upon I would …*
>
> *But screw your courage to the sticking-place.*

The King is murdered, and Macbeth becomes king; but can find no security around him, or in his own mind from his conscience. A series of murders follows; still no security, but

> *I am in blood*
> *Stepped in so far, that should I wade no*
> *more,*
> *Returning were as tedious as go o'er.*

It is curious that, while Macbeth has no redeeming feature – hardly even his love for Lady Macbeth – his personality should yet suggest a certain nobility: he has regal dignity, and perhaps even heroic stature. The solitariness of his soul at the end wrings our hearts.

Macbeth, Lady, is unlike any other woman in Shakespeare: she has no feminine qualities, she should have been a man. She it is who screws Macbeth up to murdering his King; she would have done it herself but that the King asleep made her think of her father. She has more presence of mind than Macbeth too, and manages to faint at the discovery that the King has been murdered. In the wonderful scene of Macbeth's banquet, where he is thrown off his balance by the appearance of Banquo's Ghost, she maintains self-control and almost carries it off.

Still her conscience preys upon her mind. Her sleep-walking scene is beyond anything - one can hardly bear to see it, Shakespeare so searches the crevices of the conscience, the sense of guilt in every heart. *Macbeth.*

Macduff, Scottish noble in *Macbeth*, who flies to England after the King's murder to seek help against Macbeth. There he is given the line which has become such a cliché: 'Stands Scotland where it did?' Macbeth wreaks vengeance on his wife and son. At Dunsinane, where Macbeth confronts his fate, he takes assurance in the Witches' prophecy:

> *I bear a charmèd life, which must not yield*
> *To one of woman born.*

But Macduff had not had a normal birth: he was 'from his mother's womb untimely ripped'. Macbeth falls to him, and Macduff has the satisfaction of bringing in his head at the conclusion of this grim play.

Macduff, Lady, is bitter at her husband's flight, leaving her and her children at the mercy of Macbeth. Her boy has a part, with the innocent prattle that appealed to Elizabethan taste, but which we find rather forward. *Macbeth.*

Macmorris, Irish captain in Henry V's army, his lingo taken off. *Henry V.*

Maecenas, C. Cilnius, 69–3 BC, friend of Octavius. *Antony and Cleopatra*. He was the most famous patron of the arts in antiquity - his name still in use as such. A close adviser of Octavius as Emperor Augustus.

Malcolm, son of King Duncan in *Macbeth*, who escapes to England the night of his father's murder - to return, vanquish Macbeth, and take the throne. It is given to him, during his sojourn in England, to witness Edward the Confessor's rite of healing the King's Evil:

> *A most miraculous work in this good King,*
> *Which often since my here-remain in England*
> *I have seen him do . . .*
> *To the succeeding royalty he leaves*
> *The healing benediction. With this strange*
> *virtue*
> *He hath a heavenly gift of prophecy,*
> *And sundry blessings hang about his throne,*
> *That speak him full of grace.*

This is a further compliment to James I, who, on succeeding to the English throne, after hesitating for a while as a Calvinist, took up the sacramental rite of his predecessors. The Stuarts carried it on to the last of them on the throne, Queen Anne.

Malvolio, steward to the Countess Olivia, is the most interesting character in *Twelfth Night*. Faithful to his mistress, he tries to keep order in the household, but is defeated by her uncle, Sir Toby Belch, who plots with Maria make Malvolio ridiculous. For his weakness is his self-esteem, and he is made to think that the Countess is in love with him. She thinks him mad, and he is put under restraint. Elizabethans - as Germans do - found cruelty funny; today we have more sympathy for Malvolio. That appreciative reader of Shakespeare, Charles I, thought of the play as 'Malvolio', as he noted in his copy of the Second Folio.

Mamilius, King Leontes' son, a forward child such as Elizabethans liked. *The Winter's Tale.*

Marcade, French gentleman. *Love's Labour's Lost.*

Marcellus, officer of the guard. *Hamlet.*

March, earl of, *see* Mortimer.

Marcus Andronicus, Titus's brother, tribune of the people. *Titus Andronicus.*

Mardian, attendant on Cleopatra. *Antony and Cleopatra.*

Margarelon, bastard son of King Priam. *Troilus and Cressida.*

Margaret, attendant on Hero. *Much Ado About Nothing.*

Margaret, Clarence's daughter, 1473-1541, became countess of Salisbury. Executed 1541. *Richard III.*

Margaret of Anjou, Henry VI's queen, 1430-1482. Took a partisan line as queen, identifying herself with the Lancastrian party, of which she became the leader, hostile to York and his following. Present at several battles in the Wars of the Roses, finally defeated by Edward of York at Towton, who thereupon became king. In 1471 she returned with her son Edward, Prince of

Wales, to be defeated at Tewkesbury. Imprisoned until 1476, when she retired to Anjou. In all three parts of *Henry VI*, her appearance in *Richard III* is Shakespeare's invention.

Maria, lady attendant on the Princess of France. *Love's Labour's Lost.*

Maria, waiting-woman to the Countess in *Twelfth Night*. An amusing minx, she thinks up the plot to make Malvolio ridiculous.

Mariana, of the moated grange in *Measure for Measure*. She had been betrothed to Angelo, the hypocritical Deputy, who discarded her. She substitutes - the well-worn bed-trick - for Isabella, thus saving the latter's 'honour'. Her situation in the moated grange inspired a lovely poem of Tennyson's.

Mariana, friend of the widow of Florence. *All's Well That Ends Well.*

Marina, daughter of Pericles and Thaisa, born during a storm at sea. Saved from death by pirates, she is sold to a brothel at Mytilene, where her steadfast defence of her virtue wins the respect and admiration of Lysimachus, governor of the city. These realistic brothel scenes, indubitably Shakespeare, are the best things in this romantic, experimental play. *Pericles.*

Mariner, a. *The Winter's Tale.*

Mark Antony, *see* Antony.

Marshal, a. *Pericles.*

Marshal, a lord. *Richard II.*

Martext, Sir Oliver, a vicar. *As You Like It.* The name is a take-off of the contemporary Marprelate controversy.

Martius, son of Coriolanus. *Coriolanus.*

Martius, son of Titus. *Titus Andronicus.*

Marullus, a tribune of the people, in *Julius Caesar.* He is hostile to the great man and rebukes the citizens for their devotion to him in a well-known speech:

> *Knew you not Pompey? Many a time and oft*
> *Have you climbed up to walls and*
> *battlements,*
> *To towers and windows, yea to chimney*
> *tops -*

- Elizabethan surroundings rather than Roman. It recalls the description of London's salute to Essex in Shakespeare's preceding play, *Henry V.*

Masham, *see* Scroop.

Master of a ship (a) *2 Henry VI.* (b) *The Tempest.*

Mayor (a) of Coventry, *3 Henry VI.* (b) Of St Albans, *2 Henry VI.* (c) Of York, *3 Henry VI. And see* London.

Melun, a French lord. *King John.*

Menas, follower of Octavius, had commanded a part of Sextus Pompeius' fleet against Octavius and Antony, but went over to them. *Antony and Cleopatra.*

Menecrates, friend of Sextus Pompeius. *Antony and Cleopatra.*

Menelaus, Greek prince, husband of Helen, whose abduction started the Trojan war. *Troilus and Cressida.*

Menenius Agrippa, the most attractive character in
Coriolanus, who expresses Shakespeare's point of view,
of moderation, prudence, tact. An aristocrat, friendly to
Coriolanus, he gives him the best advice and does what
he can to excuse his rough ways and lack of
consideration to the people, as those of a soldier inured
to war. In vain - Coriolanus is carried away by the force
of his own temperament; as for the people - well,
Menenius knows as well as Coriolanus what to think of
them, but is more judicious than to tell them. Instead, he
relates to them his famous parable of the Belly and the
body's other Members. Traditionally, he was a mediator
between patricians and plebeians, and ended their
conflict. He cannot bring this off in the play, hard as he
tries, because of Coriolanus's refusal to play the populist
game, and the malice of the tribunes, with whom
Menenius has a fine showdown, telling them what they
are.

Menteith, *Macbeth.*

Merchant, the, of Venice - Antonio - in the play of that
name. He stands bond, in a pound of his own flesh, for a
debt of his friend Bassanio to Shylock the Jew.
Friendship could go no further. Eventually, it is
Bassanio's mistress, Portia, who saves him by her
argument in the case at law. *Merchant of Venice.*

Merchant, First and Second, *The Comedy of Errors.*

Merchant, to Timon. *Timon of Athens.*

Mercutio, kinsman of the Prince and friend of Romeo, in
Romeo and Juliet. He is a devotee of friendship and
scorns heterosexual love. When Romeo falls again for a
woman (having first fallen for Rosaline), Mercutio laughs

at him and directs bawdy shafts which Benvolio fears
may anger him. But no, it might serve

> *To raise a spirit in his mistress' circle*
> *Of some strange nature, letting it there stand*
> *Till she had laid it and conjured it down . . .*

He teases Romeo with

> *O Romeo, that she were - O that she were*
> *An open etcetera, thou a poperin pear!*

(i.e. a Poperinghe pear).

Mercutio is given the finest passage of pure poetry in
the play, a longish poem in itself, full of native
Warwickshire folklore about Queen Mab:

> *. . . she comes*
> *In shape no bigger than an agate stone*
> *On the forefinger of an alderman.*

(Shakespeare's father was an alderman.) Then Mercutio
is killed in an affray.

Marlowe, with whom Shakespeare was closely
associated earlier, had been involved in several such
affrays, and had been slain only the year before. It is
probable that Shakespeare had Marlowe in mind in
Mercutio - even the name is suggestive, in Shakespeare's
way.

Dr Johnson reports a tradition coming from Dryden
-'which might easily reach his time', and Dryden knew
Davenant - that Shakespeare declared that 'he was
obliged to kill Mercutio in the third act, lest he should
have been killed by him'. This is very like his turn of wit;
we recall that later on he *was* obliged to kill off Falstaff
from overburdening *Henry V*.

Certainly Mercutio is a very idiosyncratic figure, no
one else quite like him in Shakespeare's work.

Messala, M. Valerius Corvinus. At Philippi he fought under

Cassius. *Julius Caesar.* Pardoned by Antony, he later joined Octavius.

Messenger, in *Much Ado About Nothing.*

Metellus Cimber, presumably brother of L. Tillius Cimber, the actual conspirator who, while presenting a petition for his brother's recall, was foremost among those gathered around Caesar to kill him. *Julius Caesar.*

Michael, a sawyer, one of Cade's rebels. *2 Henry VI.*

Michael, Sir, attendant on the archbishop of York. *1 Henry IV.* Also Cassio's first name. *See* Cassio.

Milan, duke of, father of Silvia. *The Two Gentlemen of Verona.*
   See also Antonio, Prospero.

Minola, *see* Baptista, Bianca, Katharine.

Miranda, Prospero's daughter in *The Tempest,* brought up on his enchanted isle, is unacquainted with any menfolk, naturally, and happily falls in love with shipwrecked Ferdinand, son of the King of Naples.

Montague, John Neville, marquis. *3 Henry VI.* Brother of Warwick 'the kingmaker', with him he deserted Edward IV; the two brothers were killed at Barnet, 1471. *3 Henry VI.*
   And see Salisbury.

Montague, head of the house at feud with the Capulets in Verona. An elderly man, he is content to be bound by the Prince to keep the peace. Not so the young men of both houses and their followers. *Romeo and Juliet.*

Montague, Lady, wife of Montague in *Romeo and Juliet*. She holds back her husband sensibly from brandishing his sword at old Capulet:

> *Thou shalt not stir one foot to seek a foe.*

Montano, former governor of Cyprus. *Othello*.

Montgomery, Sir John. *3 Henry VI*. Knighted 1418.

Montjoy, French herald. *Henry V*.

Moonshine, impersonated by Starveling. *A Midsummer Night's Dream*.

Moor, *see* Aaron, Morocco, Othello.

Mopsa - charming name - shepherdess. *The Winter's Tale*.

More, Sir Thomas, 1478-1535, appears in Act II.3 and III.1, which Shakespeare contributed to the corporate play, *Sir Thomas More*, where More quells the anti-immigrant riots of Evil Mayday, 1516.

Morgan, name assumed by Belarius. *Cymbeline*.

Morocco, prince of, suitor to Portia. *The Merchant of Venice*.

Mortimer, Edmund, 1376-1409?, is regarded as earl of March in *1 Henry IV*. This confuses him with his father, who was 3rd earl of March. Taken prisoner by Glendower in the Welsh resistance, he joined with him, married his daughter, and probably perished in the prolonged siege of Harlech Castle. *1 Henry IV*.

Mortimer, Lady, Glendower's daughter. *1 Henry IV*.

Mortimer, Edmund, 5th earl of March, 1391-1425. Recognised as heir by Richard II, but was loyal to the Lancastrian succession. Divulged the plot in his favour on the eve of Henry V's departure for France; made Lieutenant of Ireland, died of plague there. *1 Henry VI.*

Mortimer, Sir Hugh and Sir John, figure as uncles of Richard, duke of York, in *3 Henry VI.* Actually Sir John was knighted by Henry VII at Bosworth.

Morton, opponent of the King. *2 Henry IV.*

Morton, John, 1420-1500, bishop of Ely in *Richard III.* Afterwards cardinal, archbishop of Canterbury.

Moth, a fairy. *A Midsummer Night's Dream.*

Moth, page to Don Armado, a pert and witty youngster. *Love's Labour's Lost.*

Mouldy, Ralph, Falstaff's recruit. *2 Henry IV.*

Mowbray, in *Richard II. See* Norfolk.

Mowbray, Thomas, lord, 1386-1405, a young fool who joined Archbishop Scrope in revolt against Henry IV, captured at Bramham Moor and beheaded at nineteen. *2 Henry IV. And see* Norfolk.

Murder, character assumed by Demetrius. *Titus Andronicus.*

Murderers, the Three, in *Macbeth* offer a problem. Macbeth has employed two to murder Banquo. Who is the third who joins in? When the first reports that Banquo is dead, but his son Fleance has escaped, Macbeth says,

> *Then comes my fit again. I had else been*
> *perfect.*

This marks the point at which fortune turns against him, and he is - in a phrase contributed to the language -'cabined, cribbed, confined' by doubts and fears.

Murderers, of Clarence in *Richard III*, are distinguished from each other; the first, being more bloody, stabs Clarence, the second repents his part in the affair.
See also 2 Henry VI.

Muscovites, masque of. *Love's Labour's Lost.*

Musicians, in *Othello*, have a small speaking part.

Mustardseed, a fairy. *A Midsummer Night's Dream.*

Mutius, Titus's son whom he kills with his own hand. *Titus Andronicus.*

Myrmidons, soldiers commanded by Achilles. *Troilus and Cressida.*

Mytilene, governor of. *See* Lysimachus.

Naples, King of. *See* Alonso, Reignier.

Nathaniel (a) Sir, a curate, a figure of fun in *Love's Labour's Lost*. (b) *The Taming of the Shrew*.

Navarre, Ferdinand, king of, in *Love's Labour's Lost*. The play is a skit on the Southampton circle by its dramatist, in which Southampton figures as Navarre, abjuring the society of women. This has a doubly comic effect, for at the time Henry of Navarre was known as a devoted womaniser.

Nerissa, waiting-maid to Portia, plays the Doctor's clerk to Portia as Bellario the lawyer. *The Merchant of Venice*.

Nestor, an aged Greek prince, who expresses the wisdom of experience in *Troilus and Cressida*.

Nicanor, a Roman. *Coriolanus*.

Nicholas, *The Taming of the Shrew*.

Norfolk, John Mowbray, 4th duke and last of the Mowbray line, 1444-1476. *3 Henry VI*.

Norfolk, John Howard, 1st duke of the Howard line, ?1430-1485. He served the Yorkist cause fairly consistently and supported Richard III's usurpation, for which he was rewarded with the dukedom. Libelled

'Jockey of Norfolk', he was one of the small inner group that fought for the King at Bosworth where he was slain. *Richard III*.

Norfolk, Thomas Howard, 2nd duke of that line, 1443-1524, won the battle of Flodden against the Scots, 1513, for which Henry VIII restored him to the dukedom. An opponent of Wolsey, he had to preside at the trial of his friend and connexion, Buckingham, in 1521. *Henry VIII*.

Norfolk, Thomas Howard, 3rd duke, 1473-1554. Also an opponent of Wolsey, as later of Cromwell. Kinsman of Queen Anne Boleyn and of Queen Catherine Howard, he resigned himself to their condemnations and executions. He narrowly escaped execution himself for the indiscretions of his son, the poet Surrey. In *Henry VIII* Shakespeare does not distinguish between these two dukes, father and son, but treats them as one character. The 3rd duke's duchess appears in *Henry VIII*.

Norfolk, Thomas Mowbray, duke of, quarrels with Bolingbroke, exiled for life. *Richard II*.

Northumberland, Henry Percy, 1st earl, 1342-1408. Joined Bolingbroke in 1399 and supported his call to the throne; later quarrelled with him as King Henry IV and supported his son, Harry Hotspur's, rebellion, but was not present at the battle of Shrewsbury and was pardoned. Conspired with Glendower and Mortimer, rebelled, fled into Scotland, invaded England, slain at Bramham Moor. *Richard II* and *1* and *2 Henry IV*.

Northumberland, Lady. *2 Henry IV*. In historic fact Northumberland was a widower by this time.

Northumberland, Henry Percy, 2nd earl, 1394-1455. A Lancastrian, fell at St Albans fighting against York. *3 Henry VI*.

Northumberland, Henry Percy, 3rd earl 1421-1461. A
Lancastrian, defeated Yorkists at Wakefield and St
Albans; slain at Towton. *3 Henry VI.*
See also Siward.

Norway, Prince of, *see* Fortinbras.

Norwegian captain. *Hamlet.*

Nurse, the, in *Romeo and Juliet* is a wonderful creation, a
transcript from real life with some caricature. She is very
human, quite inconstant; though she expects to be
respected, and is highly indignant at the young men
making fun of her, she has no moral stance properly
speaking. She is ready to aid Romeo's surreptitious
access to the young lady in her charge; when he is
banished, she goes over to the other suitor, the Count
Paris:

> *O, he's a lovely gentleman.*
> *Romeo's a dishclout to him; an eagle, madam,*
> *Hath not so green, so quick, so fair an eye*
> *As Paris hath, etc.*

She is very down-to-earth, with a relish for bawdy talk.
   Dr Johnson, a real writer, had the perception to see
that the Nurse's part is one of those that gave
Shakespeare pure pleasure to depict. As for her
character, 'He has, with great subtlety of distinction,
drawn her at once loquacious and secret, obsequious and
insolent, trusty and dishonest.' She loves her charge, but
like such types cannot stick to one line - Shakespeare
knew well how little consistency there is in humans.
   The Nurse's much-quoted lines,

> *'Tis since the earthquake now eleven years ...*
> *Shake, quoth the dove-house,*

refer to the earthquake of 1583. Everything points to

1594 as the play's date, 'in proximity to *A Midsummer Night's Dream*', as Sisson says. Both are related to the Southampton period, so decisive in Shakespeare's life.

Nurse, to Tamora's black child. *Titus Andronicus.*

Nurse, a, *3 Henry VI.*

Nym, Corporal, follower of Falstaff. *2 Henry IV, Henry V, The Merry Wives of Windsor.*

Nymphs, in the masque. *The Tempest.*

Oatcake, Hugh. *Much Ado About Nothing*.

Oberon, king of the fairies. *A Midsummer Night's Dream*.

Octavia, sister of Octavius Caesar, who was very fond of her and gave her in marriage to Antony. She was more beautiful than Cleopatra, but chaste and virtuous, and could not hold Antony who had always liked dissipation. On returning to Egypt and Cleopatra, Antony in fact divorced Octavia. This does not appear in the play, nor - naturally - that after Antony's death she nobly brought up his children with those by his first wife Fulvia and by Cleopatra. *Antony and Cleopatra*.

Octavius Caesar, 63 BC-AD 14, is known by this name in *Julius Caesar* and in *Antony and Cleopatra*, better known in history as the Emperor Augustus. The great-nephew of Julius Caesar, he was adopted as his heir, and turned out to have just the qualities required to inherit Caesar's position in the state. Mark Antony expected to succeed to it, but was outmatched by the younger man's cool and wise political judgment. After Caesar's death Octavius formed an alliance with Antony and Lepidus, the Triumvirs, to divide and rule the Roman world between them. Later, this broke apart, as we see portrayed in *Antony and Cleopatra*. In both plays Antony has a larger, more dramatic and popular part. Nevertheless, Octavius emerges as the master, for he has overmastering political judgment. Though this type is less popular, Shakespeare understood it and the necessity of its rôle in politics and in history - as sentimental critics, like Hazlitt, rarely do.

Moreover, Octavius has the Caesarean quality of magnanimity: on the news of Antony's death he pronounces:

> ... the death of Antony
> Is not a single doom: in the name lay
> A moiety of the world.

Officers play the part of a chorus in *Coriolanus*, commenting on the action, much to the purpose. The Second Officer: 'There have been many great men that have flattered the people, who ne'er loved them; and there be many that they have loved, they know not wherefore. So that if they love they know not why, they hate upon no better a ground.'

The first Officer thereupon passes a shrewd judgment upon Coriolanus, for all his bravery: 'To seem to affect the malice and displeasure of the people is as bad as that which he dislikes, to flatter them for their love.'

Officers, First and Second. *Twelfth Night.*

Old Lady, attending upon Queen Katharine. *Henry VIII.*

Old Man of the Capulet household. *Romeo and Juliet.*

Old Man, in *King Lear*, is a tenant of Gloucester and leads him on his way when blinded.

Old Man, in *Macbeth*, reflects on the unnatural portents the night of Duncan's murder.

Oliver, eldest son of Sir Rowland de Boys, unkind brother of Orlando. *As You Like It.*

113

Olivia, the Countess, in *Twelfth Night* rejects the suit of the Duke of Illyria, but falls for his intermediary, Viola, disguised as a youth. She is eventually consoled with Viola's brother, Sebastian.

Ophelia, daughter of Polonius, in *Hamlet*, and sister of Laertes, who seeks to revenge her death upon Hamlet, whom he holds responsible for it - as he was. For he really loved her and gave her to think so, then treated her with all the greater cruelty in his own distraction, because he suspects that her father is using her to spy on him on behalf of his uncle, the King. Thus Ophelia is driven to real madness and drowns herself - the most touching victim in all Shakespeare: the rendering of Hamlet's cruel treatment of her - so penetrating psychologically - and her madness, beyond anything in the history of the stage.

Hamlet's mother, the Queen, strewing flowers upon her grave:

Sweets to the sweet, farewell.

Orlando, hero of *As You Like It*, whose pursuit of Rosalind, the exiled Duke's daughter in the Forest of Arden makes the play.

Orléans, the Bastard of. *1 Henry VI*.

Orléans, duke of, Charles, 1391-1465. Captured at Agincourt when twenty-four, he was for years prisoner in England, where he wrote much of his poetry. Married Richard II's young widow. *Henry V*.

Orléans, master gunner of, with his son. *1 Henry VI*.

Orsino, duke of Illyria, melancholy on account of his unavailing suit for the Countess Olivia. *Twelfth Night*.

Osric, a young Court fop, brings a message from the King to Hamlet. Once more a realistic caricature: there were such types at the Elizabethan Court, with which Shakespeare was so familiar from constant acting there. Described as a 'waterfly', he is the butt of Hamlet's scoriating wit. *Hamlet*.

Ostler, *see* Tom.

Oswald, Goneril's steward in *King Lear*, a nasty type who serves her ill purposes and is railed upon by good old Kent. His challenge, 'if I had thee in Lipsbury pinfold, I would make thee care for me', is an unexplained crux, much discussed; it means no more than 'if I had you between my teeth'. For this Kent was disgracefully put in the stocks - and he an earl!

Othello, hero of the play of that name, for he is of heroic stature. Though he was 'thick-lipped' and of 'sooty bosom', he was not a black but a Moor. Nevertheless, his marriage to Desdemona broke the conventions, angered her father, and led to tragedy. We see again - as with anti-Semitism in *The Merchant of Venice* - that Shakespeare was concerned with questions we think of as modern: in this case race-relations.

For indeed these are at the back of the tragedy - Desdemona does not really understand her hero, nor he her, though they passionately love each other. Too much so - it is a tragedy of love - for it opens Othello to extreme jealousy; his suspicious nature is wrought on, his innocence taken advantage of. Similarly, Desdemona is too confident in her innocence and love; thus she becomes a victim.

The play, first performed at Court on 1 November 1604, was a favourite with Dr Johnson, for all its romantic *fougue*. 'The beauties of this play impress themselves so strongly upon the attention of the reader

115

that they can draw no aid from critical illustration.' (If only lesser critics would realise that!) 'The fiery openness of Othello, magnanimous, artless and credulous, boundless in his confidence, ardent in his affection, inflexible in his resolution, and obdurate in his revenge . . .'

Perhaps we may add something factual to this: his services to the state had been exceptional and merited exceptional consideration. Nevertheless he might not have got away with his noble bride, if it had not been for the critical situation with which the play begins. The Turkish threat to Cyprus demanded Othello's immediate presence and command.

This was a situation with which Elizabethans were all too familiar - with the advance of the Turks in the Mediterranean - and the urgency of which they could appreciate.

Outlaws. *The Two Gentlemen of Verona.*

Overdone, Mistress, a brothel-madam. An engaging contemporary caricature: 'what with the war, what with the sweat ['flu epidemic], what with the gallows, and what with poverty, I am custom-shrunk'. *Measure for Measure.*

Oxford, John de Vere, 13th earl, 1443-1513; helped to restore Henry VI in 1470, seized St Michael's Mount 1473, commanded Richmond's army at Bosworth 1485. *3 Henry VI, Richard III.*

Page, to Mariana in the moated grange, sings the lovely song

> *Take, O take those lips away*
> *That so sweetly were forsworn.*
> *Measure for Measure.*

Page, to Count Paris, in *Romeo and Juliet*, has two engaging lines:

> *I am almost afraid to stand alone*
> *Here in the churchyard, yet I will adventure.*

He witnesses the fight between Romeo and Count Paris, and calls the Watch.

Page, to the countess of Rousillon. *All's Well That Ends Well.*

Page, Anne, the Pages' pretty daughter, whom Dr Caius and Slender are after, but young Master Fenton wins her. *The Merry Wives of Windsor.*

Page, George, townsman of Windsor, annoyed by Falstaff's proposals to his wife, takes part in exposing him. He has the tell-tale line, *à propos* of Nym's constant use of the word 'humour', recently patented by Ben Jonson: 'The humour of it, quoth' a. Here's a fellow frights English out of his wits.' *The Merry Wives of Windsor.*

Page, Mistress, takes a merry part with Mistress Ford in fooling the libidinous Falstaff. *The Merry Wives of Windsor.*

Page, young William, is given a Latin lesson by the Welsh curate in *The Merry Wives of Windsor*. There is more about schoolmasters and teaching in Shakespeare than other dramatists, to corroborate John Aubrey's information that for a time he was an usher in the country.

Painter, a, flatters Timon for his patronage, and engages in a good deal of artistic patter with the Poet. All very contemporary. *Timon of Athens.*

Palmer, Sir Thomas, d. 1553. *Sir Thomas More.*

Pandar, a, provides Marina for the brothel in *Pericles*, but is disappointed of his expectations.

Pandarus in *Troilus and Cressida* is her uncle and fixes her up with Troilus. He gives name to the profession of pandar.

Pandulph, legate from Pope Innocent III to King John. He eventually secured a truce between King and revolting barons. *King John.*

Panthino, servant to Antonio. *The Two Gentlemen of Verona.*

Paris, governor of. *1 Henry VI.*

Paris, son of King Priam of Troy, who caused the Trojan war by abducting Helen from Greece, and of course advocates keeping her against his father's better judgment. Paris's arguments sound implausible, but he is supported by Troilus, another young fool. Hence came the destruction of Troy. *Troilus and Cressida.*

Paris, Count, kinsman of the Prince of Verona. *Romeo and Juliet*. Juliet's father, Capulet, insists on her marrying him - unaware that she is already married to Romeo. When laid in her vault, thinking her dead, her suitor goes to say farewell, and there encounters Romeo. In the fight Paris is slain.

Parolles, follower of Count Bertram in *All's Well That Ends Well*. A remarkable character, caricature of the braggart soldier of the time, a transcript from contemporary life. His showing-up as poltroon and liar, by his fellows in the army, makes the chief comedy in this serious play. Yet - 'Simply the thing I am shall make me live.'
  Southampton had a braggadocio captain, one Edmonds, with whom he would play and 'cull' in his tent in Ireland, while Essex took him about in his coach. Shakespeare had observed the type.

Patchbreech, fisherman. *Pericles*.

Patience, waiting-woman to Queen Katharine. *Henry VIII*.

Patroclus, Greek, bosom friend of Achilles. Together they sulk in their tent; only when Patroclus ventures forth and is killed is the mighty Achilles roused to revenge his death upon Hector. *Troilus and Cressida*. (Something of Essex and Southampton is glanced at here; Essex would sulk in his tent when he could not get his way with Queen Elizabeth, and was accompanied by Southampton.)

Paulina, wife to Antigonus, faithful attendant of Leontes' queen, for whom she stands up to him. A splendid outspoken character. *The Winter's Tale*.

Peaseblossom, a fairy. *A Midsummer Night's Dream*.

Pedant, a. *The Taming of the Shrew*.

119

Pedro, *see* Don Pedro.

Pembroke, William the Marshall, earl of Pembroke, d. 1231. Supporting John for the throne, he ruled the country in the King's absence abroad, and was guardian of his son, Prince Henry, afterwards Henry III.

Pembroke, William Herbert, 1st earl of that line. Yorkist, was awarded Jasper Tudor's earldom and the guardianship of young Richmond, afterwards Henry VII. Captured and executed by Lancastrians at Edgecote. *3 Henry VI.*

Percy, Henry, surnamed Hotspur, 1364–1403, eldest son of 1st earl of Northumberland; assisted his father to place Henry IV on the throne, but became dissatisfied and revolted, slain at the battle of Shrewsbury. Appears briefly in *Richard II*, an important character in *1 Henry IV*, where Shakespeare makes him a younger man, coeval with Prince Henry for dramatic contrast. A hasty, impulsive type, of down-to-earth common sense, he cannot stand Glendower's mystical Celtic nonsense, and has no political sense himself.

Percy, Lady, Hotspur's wife, was historically the daughter of Edmund Mortimer, 3rd earl of March. *1* and *2 Henry IV.*
   And see Northumberland, Worcester.

Perdita, daughter of King Leontes, discarded by him, brought up by an old shepherd in Bohemia, where Prince Florizel is destined to fall for her. *The Winter's Tale.*

Pericles, prince of Tyre, chief character of the play of that name – an experimental play of which Shakespeare wrote the last three Acts, and probably shaped or supervised the first two. The play is like a picaresque novel, in which

Pericles has a succession of adventures, escaping death by land and sea; gaining a wife at a foreign court, losing her in a storm at sea. She is presumed dead and, coffined, lands on a coast, restored to life. Reunion and happiness all round at the end of this tragi-comedy or romance.

Peter of Pomfret (i.e. Pontefract), a prophet. *King John.*

Peter, has a pretty part in *Romeo and Juliet* in attending upon Juliet's Nurse, and also singing:

> *Musicians, O musicians, Heart's Ease,*
> *Heart's Ease.*
> *O, an you will have me live, play Heart's*
> *Ease -*

one of the most popular of Elizabethan tunes: to which he sings one of the songs of Richard Edwards.
And see Friar Peter.

Peto, one of Falstaff's followers. *1* and *2 Henry IV.*

Petruchio, a Capulet follower. *Romeo and Juliet.*

Petruchio, gentleman of Verona, tamer of the Shrew. *The Taming of the Shrew.* A splendid, rumbustious character, he breaks her in, like a colt, by a combination of firmness and affection - also showing her what a fool she has been. She learns.

Phebe, shepherdess. *As You Like It.*

Philario, friend of Leonatus in Rome. He brings along Iachimo, with whom Leonatus makes the silly wager to prove his wife's chastity, and is thereby deceived. *Cymbeline.*

Philarmonus, *see* Soothsayer in *Cymbeline.*

121

Philemon, servant to Cerimon. *Pericles*.

Philip, *The Taming of the Shrew*.

Philip II, of France, 1165-1223, one of the ablest of medieval kings and King John's successful opponent, who conquered Normandy and other territories John had inherited in France. Philip recognises Arthur as Richard Coeur-de-lion's successor, then in Shakespeare's play, *King John*, is made to desert the lad for political advantage ('Commodity'). He cooperated with the baronial opposition to John, and planned the invasion of England by the Dauphin Louis. *King John*.

Philip the Bastard, *see* Faulconbridge.

Philo, follower of Antony. *Antony and Cleopatra*.

Philostrate, master of the revels to Theseus. *A Midsummer Night's Dream*.

Philotus, servant of a Timon creditor. *Timon of Athens*.

Phrynia (Phryne), one of Alcibiades' two whores in *Timon of Athens*. One of the most beautiful women in antiquity, she was much sculpted and painted. Timon charges these ladies with spreading venereal disease - a contemporary note: cf. my *Simon Forman: Sex and Society in Shakespeare's Age*.

Pilch, fisherman. *Pericles*.

Pinch, a caricature of a schoolmaster. *The Comedy of Errors*.

Pindarus, servant to Cassius. *Julius Caesar*.

Pirates play a part in *Pericles*.

Pisanio, in *Cymbeline*, servant of Leonatus, Imogen's husband. Convinced by false evidence of his wife's betrayal of him and her honour with Iachimo, Leonatus orders Pisanio to kill her. He is no less convinced of her innocence, and accompanies her faithfully in her flight to Wales, where they all meet up at the end.

Pistol, 'ancient or ensign', follower of Falstaff. *2 Henry IV, Henry V, The Merry Wives of Windsor*.

Players in *Hamlet*. The production of a play not only exposes King Claudius's crime but provides an opportunity for Shakespeare to express his professional ideas as to acting. An invaluable insight into his work as producer, as well as his comments on the rivalry at the time between the Men's Companies and the Boys', for whom Ben Jonson was then writing and was their protagonist.

Players, who are to perform *The Taming of the Shrew*, are welcomed by the Lord in the Induction, who commands them to be entertained in the buttery - as Shakespeare would have been as a touring player.

Poet, the, a fascinating portrayal in *Timon of Athens*, really of the contemporary writer seeking patronage from a lord - which Shakespeare knew all about from personal experience.
And see Cinna.

Poins, Ned, follower of Prince Henry and Falstaff, *1* and *2 Henry IV*.

Polixenes, King of Bohemia, of whom his early friend King Leontes develops a mad jealousy. *The Winter's Tale*.

Polonius, chief councillor to Claudius, king of Denmark, prosy, interfering busybody, who is the butt of Hamlet's brilliant sarcastic wit. For all that, Polonius is no fool, though he cannot see through Hamlet - that no one can, except perhaps his father, the Ghost. Polonius is King Claudius's confidant and lends himself to the King's purposes to spy on Hamlet. Thus he got his comeuppance, stabbed while listening behind the arras.

Several flecks of old Lord Burghley - to whom the Essex-Southampton group were hostile - are discernible in the caricature-portrait of Polonius, to those who know the situation at Elizabeth's Court in these years. Burghley had died in 1598; *Hamlet* was written in 1600. Shakespeare's handling of the topical is characteristically oblique.

Dr Johnson appreciated the political essence of Polonius's character well. 'Polonius is a man bred in Courts, exercised in business, stored with observation, confident of his knowledge, proud of his eloquence, and declining into dotage... This idea of encroaching upon wisdom will solve all the phenomena of the character of Polonius.' It also stands for Burghley very well, constantly complaining of his ailments in his last years. For some time the target of Essex, butt of the younger men (for he stood in their way), he died in 1598. In 1600 he could be reflected upon, in Shakespeare's oblique way - as there are flecks too of Essex playing around the portrayal of Hamlet.

Polydore, the name given to Guiderius.

Pompeius, Sextus, *see* Sextus.

Pompey, a pimp, servant to Mistress Overdone - his lower-class talk is of Shakespearean virtuosity in realistic caricature. *Measure for Measure.*

Pompey the Great, impersonated by Costard. *Love's Labour's Lost.*

Popilius Lena (Laenas), a senator in *Julius Caesar.*

Porter, the, in *Macbeth* supplies the only comic relief in that sombre yet lurid tragedy - in his answer to the celebrated knocking at the gate on the night of King Duncan's murder. Not only that, but his speech links the play with the Gunpowder Plot, with his play on equivocation. 'Faith, here's an equivocator that could swear against both the scales in either scale, who committed treason enough for God's sake ... O come in, equivocator.' etc.

This was an appeal to popular feeling against the Jesuit doctrine of equivocation. At the trial of the Gunpowder Plotters, the Jesuit Provincial, Henry Garnet, explained his equivocation: he had heard of the Plot, but under the seal of confession could not impart his knowledge as a warning. This made the worst possible impression; and Shakespeare, representing the public's view, refers to the treason yet again.

Porter (a) *2 Henry IV.* (b) *I Henry VI.*

Porter, with his man. *Henry VIII.*

Porter, Gentleman, of the Tower. *Sir Thomas More.*

Portia, the rich heiress in *The Merchant of Venice*, for whose hand two princes contend, but the prize is won by the Merchant's friend Bassanio - for whom the Merchant has given his bloody bond to Shylock. In return, disguised as the lawyer Bellario, Portia saves the Merchant's life in the trial of his case with Shylock.

Portia was a favourite character with the Victorians, her speeches - 'The quality of mercy is not strained', etc.

- rapturously received. Evidently sentiment was stronger in Victorian hearts than in our disillusioned days.

Portia (Porcia), in *Julius Caesar*, Brutus's wife. She was the daughter of the Stoic Cato. Brutus's love for her is a redeeming feature, and gives him the most affecting of his lines: she is

> As dear to me as are the ruddy drops
> That visit my sad heart.

He promises to reveal to her what makes him sad, the secret of the conspiracy, 'by and by'; in historical fact he trusted her with it the night before the assissination. Historically, she comitted suicide *after* Brutus's death at Philippi; but placing it before, imparting the news to Cassius, helps to make it the most humanly moving scene in the play. She 'swallowed fire' probably refers to a fairly common mode of suicide with ancient Romans -inhaling charcoal fumes.

Posthumus Leonatus in *Cymbeline* is beloved by Imogen, the King's daughter, who marries him though he is greatly beneath her in station and has to fly the realm. In Rome he makes a wager with Iachimo to prove his wife's chastity in his absence, and falls victim to the scheming Italian's deceit. The rest of the play has to put this right.

Potpan, servant to Capulet. *Romeo and Juliet.*

Prat, Mother, character assumed by Falstaff. *See* Brentford.

Priam, King of Troy. *Troilus and Cressida.*

Priest, a. *Twelfth Night.*

Proculeius, C., friend of Octavius, whom he sent after the deplorable couple after Actium. *Antony and Cleopatra.*

Prospero, exiled duke of Milan in *The Tempest.* In his enchanted isle (Shakespeare had Bermuda in mind) he is a magus, has enslaved the savage Caliban, the previous proprietor, and has the spirit Ariel at command. He also has a daughter. The play was sparked off by the wreck of the *Sea Venture* on Bermuda, the account of which came back to Blackfriars, where Shakespeare was part owner of the theatre.

The play was next to his last. Now that we realise that Shakespeare was the most autobiographical of Elizabethan dramatists, we need not doubt that he had himself in mind in writing:

> *Our revels now are ended. These our actors . . .*
> *Are melted into air, into thin air;*
> *And like the baseless fabric of this vision*
> *The cloud-capped towers, the gorgeous*
> *   palaces,*
> *The solemn temples, the great globe itself . . .*

- one sees the palaces and towers of Elizabethan London, and the Globe Theatre on the south bank of the Thames -

> *. . . shall dissolve,*
> *And like this insubstantial pageant faded*
> *Leave not a rack behind.*

Proteus, one of *The Two Gentlemen of Verona*, who ultimately gets his friend's girl, Silvia; though Valentine warns him:

> *And writers say, as the most forward bud*
> *Is eaten by the canker ere it blow -*
> *Even so by love the young and tender wit*
> *Is turned to folly, blasting in the bud,*

127

> *Losing his verdure even in the prime,*
> *And all the fair effects of future hopes.*

Shakespeare is the writer who says precisely this in the Sonnets, the same images, warning the young patron that he may be made a fool of and blast the hopes formed of him.

Provost, the, has quite a part in *Measure for Measure*.

Publius, senator in *Julius Caesar*.

Publius, son of Marcus Andronicus. *Titus Andronicus*.

Puck, or Robin Goodfellow, an enchanting creation straight out of country folklore. 'Are not you he/That frights the maidens of the villagery ...?' etc. In *A Midsummer Night's Dream* he is attendant upon Oberon, king of the fairies, who employs him to dose Titania with love-juice - hence her infatuation for an ass - as also the young lovers. He is the instrument of the confusions of the play.

Queen, the, in *Cymbeline* is unnamed, the King's second wife, mother of Cloten by a former husband. She is a wicked stepmother to Imogen, whom - when she rejects Cloten - the Queen tries to poison. She procures a draught from her doctor, on the pretence that it is for animals, 'creatures not worth the hanging'. Even so he replies, she

> *Shall from this practice but make hard your heart.*

She has a hard heart, ambitious, scheming, of the race of evil women such as Goneril or Regan. But she is in contrast to them: she is subtler, a hypocrite, playing the part of all kindness to Imogen in the King's presence, who is taken in by her - not Imogen however, another woman.

Quickly, Mistress, hostess of the Boar's Head in East Cheap, *1* and *2 Henry IV*. In *Henry V* she married Pistol, but reappears as Mistress Quickly in *The Merry Wives of Windsor*. Mistress also of malapropisms, was she their patentee on the stage?

Quince, Peter, carpenter. *A Midsummer Night's Dream*.

Quintus, son of Titus. *Titus Andronicus*.

Ragozine, head of. *Measure for Measure*.

Ralph, servant in *The Taming of the Shrew*.

Rambures, French lord. *Henry V*.

Rapine, character assumed by Chiron. *Titus Andronicus*.

Ratcliffe, Sir Richard. Agent of Richard III, killed at Bosworth, 1485. *Richard III*.

Reapers, in the masque. *The Tempest*.

Rebeck, Hugh, musician. *Romeo and Juliet*.

Regan, Lear's second daughter, married to the Duke of Cornwall who aids and abets her in wrongdoing. She helps to bind Gloucester while her husband blinds him. A faithful servant fatally wounds Cornwall; Regan kills him. In this exciting sub-plot, her husband's death gives her the edge over her sister and the hope of marrying him. Goneril counters this by poisoning her. What is there to choose between them? Even Edmund, who has sworn his love to both, does not know. *King Lear*.

Reignier (René), duke of Anjou, 1409-1480, father of Margaret, Henry VI's queen. *1 Henry VI*.

Richard II, 1367-1400, son of the Black Prince and Joan, the 'Fair Maid of Kent', whose feminine looks and pleasure-loving temperament he inherited. Richard succeeded his grandfather, Edward III, in 1377 at the age of ten. First married to Anne of Bohemia, who died in 1394, two years later he married Isabella of France, then a child of seven, as part of his peace policy. The long war with France left a legacy of unrest and exacting taxation. On attaining his majority Richard's personal rule added to his difficulties by his preference for favourites and his extravagance. The magnates overthrew his rule and proscribed his friends at the 'Merciless Parliament' of 1389.

A turn in the wheel of fortune enabled Richard to recover power, and eventually wreak his revenge upon his opponents, increasing instability by his arbitrary rule. Lancaster's heir, Bolingbroke, and Norfolk accused each other of treason; Richard exiled Bolingbroke for ten years, Norfolk for life. On the death of John of Gaunt Richard seized the vast Lancastrian inheritance into his own hands, creating a sense of insecurity throughout the propertied classes, besides the injustice of it. He thereupon left for Ireland, leaving the coast clear for Bolingbroke's return to claim his own. Events forced him to take the throne; Richard was in a psychotic state in his last years of rule and would have to be replaced. Richard returned to find the country against him, power in the hands of his opponent. Having resigned the crown, he was relegated to Pontefract Castle, where he met his fate in February 1400, no one knows precisely how.

Shakespeare's play concentrates on the events of Richard's last two years as king. His rendering of Richard's un-adult emotional instability is veracious enough. A medieval king needed to be a tough - and Richard was no fighting man. He was something of an aesthete, devoted to display, the cultivated arts, and building; thus his extravagance had some offsetting advantage, for he rebuilt Westminster Hall in splendour. *Richard II.*

Richard II's queen, *see* Isabel.

Richard III, 1452-1485, youngest son of Richard, duke of York. After Tewkesbury, Henry VI was murdered in the Tower of London, when Richard was known to be there. Marrying Warwick's daughter Anne, he quarrelled bitterly with his brother Clarence over the inheritance. He ruled the North for Edward IV, on whose death he seized power, defeating the Queen's party and getting her sons, Edward V and Richard, into his power. They were never seen again after August 1483. Recognised as Protector, he was aided in his plans by Buckingham, but Edward IV's friend, Hastings, refused to go along with him and was summarily executed.

He had Edward IV declared illegitimate, to the grief of his mother; his usurpation further alienated support. In the autumn of 1483 there were risings against his rule in the southern counties, and Buckingham revolted, but was defeated, and executed at Salisbury. Richard's only son now died, followed shortly by his queen. Richard considered marrying his niece, Elizabeth, now the Yorkist heiress, but was humiliatingly forced by the city of London to swear that he had no such intention.

He had turned the country's stomach; half the Yorkist party went over to the Lancastrian heir, Henry Tudor, abroad. When Henry invaded in August 1485, Richard was taken by surprise. At Bosworth he had twice the number of Henry's forces, but one half of his army would not fight for him. Only his own cronies joined him in a desperate charge, when the forces led by the Stanleys decided the issue and Richard was killed. His body was treated humiliatingly - as no anointed king would have been but for his 'heinous crime', the words of a descendant of his supporter, the Duke of Norfolk, who knew the family tradition.

Richard dominates the play of his name, and also appears under his earlier title, Duke of Gloucester, in *2* and *3 Henry VI*. Shakespeare's portrayal of him is roughly in keeping with historical fact and his authorities; but he makes him more interesting, adding an element of malicious glee in wrong-doing. In fact Richard was a morose character with none of the charm of his handsome brothers, Edward IV and Clarence. The early soubriquet 'Crouchback' testifies to some physical defect.

Richard, 3rd duke of York. *See* York.

Richard, duke of York, 1472-1483, second son of Edward IV. When his uncle, Richard of Gloucester, took the young king Edward V in his custody to the Tower, their mother took Richard into sanctuary in Westminster Abbey, but was forced to let him join his brother in the Tower. They were never seen again after August 1483. *Richard III.*

Richmond, Henry Tudor, earl of, afterwards Henry VII, posthumous son of Edmund Tudor, earl of Richmond, and Margaret Beaufort, heiress of the Lancastrian royal House. On Edward IV's return in 1471 Henry went into exile in Brittany, and upon Richard III's usurpation and murder of the Princes in the Tower Henry became the candidate of disaffected Yorkists as well. He swore a solemn oath to heal the breach by marrying the Yorkist heiress, Elizabeth.

In 1485 he landed at Milford Haven with 2000 French mercenaries, marching through Wales gathering support, to defeat Richard III at Bosworth Field. Immediately recognised as king, he married Elizabeth of York next year: it turned out a happy marriage. He secured the alliance of Spain with the marriage of his son Arthur to Katharine of Aragon; and married his daughter Margaret to James IV of Scotland, through which the eventual unity of Britain was achieved and from which the present royal House descends. His memory is preserved to us in the magnificent Henry VII's Chapel he built on to Westminster Abbey. In Shakespeare he makes his appearance in *Richard III* as Richmond.

Rinaldo, servant to the countess of Rousillon. *All's Well That Ends Well.*

Rivers, Anthony Woodville, 2nd earl, 1442-1483. A Lancastrian, but transferred his allegiance to Edward IV, who married his sister Elizabeth. A highly cultivated man, whose translations from French were published by Caxton. Rivers was in favour with Edward IV, on whose death Richard of Gloucester had him executed. *3 Henry VI* and *Richard III.*

Robert, *Merry Wives of Windsor.*

Robin (a) *2 Henry VI.* (b) Page to Falstaff. *The Merry Wives of Windsor.*

Robin Goodfellow, *see* Puck.

Rochester, bishop of, John Fisher. *Henry VIII, Sir Thomas More.*

Roderigo, a gentleman of Venice, suitor for Desdemona's hand, whom her father has rejected. But in Cyprus, Iago lures him on with the hope - credulous fool - of obtaining her favours:

> *If thou canst cuckold him* [*Othello*], *thou dost thyself a pleasure, me a sport.*

And Iago uses him further to quarrel with and wound Cassio. In the course of his campaign Iago speaks several home truths, which serve only to fascinate

Roderigo, like a snake a rabbit. It is impossible to have any sympathy for such a fool - and of course Iago has no pity or mercy for such. *Othello.*

Rogero, *The Winter's Tale.*

Roman Captain. *Cymbeline.*

Roman Herald. *Coriolanus.*

Rome, emperor of, *see* Saturninus.

Romeo, hero of the lyrical tragedy, *Romeo and Juliet.* He is the son of Montague, head of the rival house of Capulet, at feud with each other in Verona. Romeo and Juliet fall passionately in love with each other - a fatal passion considering the mortal hatred between the houses and their respective followers. Thus they are 'star-crossed' lovers from the first to their affecting ends.

Professor C.J. Sisson remarks perceptively that: 'It is notable that we see so little in Shakespeare of the prevailing attitude of his fellow-dramatists towards Italy, which presents a land and people of Machiavellian villainy, of poison and assassination, the Circe of nations.' For Shakespeare, Italy was associated above all with love. And there was reason for that in his own passionate and troubled involvement with Emilia Bassano, Mrs Lanier - especially about the time of those plays with an Italian flavouring, *The Two Gentlemen of Verona* and *Romeo and Juliet* of 1592 and 1594; reflected later in *The Merchant of Venice* of 1596 and *Much Ado* of 1599. He had the art of making a little go a very long way.

Dr Johnson: 'This play is one of the most pleasing of our author's performances. The scenes are busy and various, the incidents numerous and important, the catastrophe irresistibly affecting; and the process of the action carried on with such probability - at least with such congruity to popular opinions - as tragedy requires.'

Actually, the idea of placing a story of passionate young love in the fatal ambience of family feud was suggested by events in which Southampton was closely involved: the fatal feud between his friends, the Danvers brothers, and the Longs in Wiltshire, which culminated in the murder of Henry Long, the heir, in the autumn of 1593. The play belongs to 1594. *See* my *Shakespeare's Southampton.*

Roper, Margaret and William. *Sir Thomas More.*

Rosalind, daughter of Duke Senior, dearest friend of Celia, usurping Duke's daughter: her courtship by Orlando is the stuff of *As You Like It.*

Rosaline, lady attending on the Princess of France in *Love's Labour's Lost* - a skit on Southampton and his circle. She is described in practically the same words as the Dark Lady (Emilia Lanier) is in the Sonnets, who was known in the circle. In the play Rosaline pairs off, rightly, with Berowne (i.e. Shakespeare).

Rosencrantz had been, with Guildenstern, a fellow-student with Hamlet at Wittenberg and friendly with him. They return to the Court of Denmark and lend themselves to the King's purpose to spy on him and betray him. His cross-questioning and exposure of them is brilliantly done. When Claudius sends Hamlet to England they carry the commission for his execution there. Hamlet discovers it and they meet their fate instead.

These false friends provide a striking contrast with Horatio, most faithful of friends to Hamlet.

Ross, lord, in *Richard II.* He would be William, 6th lord Ross, d. 1414.

Ross, Scottish noble in *Macbeth*, who tries to comfort Lady Macduff on her husband's flight to England. Later he bears thither the news of her and her children's slaughter by the tyrant, and returns to take part in his destruction at Dunsinane.

Rousillon, countess of, the, in *All's Well That Ends Well*, mother of the spoiled young Count Bertram, is a charming character - as was indeed Southampton's mother. And she favours her son's marrying - as too did the Countess of Southampton. Bernard Shaw thought the Countess the most charming woman in all Shakespeare - going pretty far, just like Shaw.

Rumour, presenter of the play. *2 Henry IV.*

Rutland, Edmund, earl of, second son of Richard, 3rd duke of York, killed as a youth with his father at Sandal near Wakefield. He appears with his tutor. *3 Henry VI.*

Sailors, *Hamlet, Othello, Pericles.*

St Albans, mayor of. *2 Henry VI.*

St Asaph, bishop of. *Henry VIII.*

Salerio, friend of Antonio the Merchant. *The Merchant of Venice.*

Salisbury, William Longespée (Longsword), earl of, d. 1226, a natural son of Henry II. One of the barons who counselled King John to grant the Great Charter. Joined the Dauphin Louis on his invasion, but returned to the English allegiance after John's death. One sees his tomb in Salisbury cathedral. *King John.*

Salisbury, John Montagu, 3rd earl, *c.* 1350-1400, accompanied Richard II to Ireland; conspired against Henry IV, killed by a mob at Cirencester. *Richard II.*

Salisbury, Thomas Montagu, 4th earl, 1388-1428, active in the war in France, besieged Orléans; killed by a cannon-ball. *1 Henry VI.*

Salisbury, Richard Neville, 1st earl of that line, 1400-60. *2 Henry VI.*

Sampson, servant to Capulet. *Romeo and Juliet.*

Sandys, lord, William, 1st baron, d. 1540. *Henry VIII.*

Saturninus, emperor of Rome, marries Tamora, queen of the Goths, enemy of Titus. *Titus Andronicus.*

Satyrs, dance of. *The Winter's Tale.*

Sawyer, a. *2 Henry VI.*

Say, James Fiennes, lord Say and Sele, *c.* 1395-1450, unpopular as Lord Treasurer, beheaded by Cade's rebels. *2 Henry VI.*

Scales, Thomas, 7th lord, *c.* 1399-1460, commander against Cade's rebels, murdered by the mob in London. *2 Henry VI.*

Scarus, (M. Scaurus), friend of Antony. *Antony and Cleopatra.* Historically, he betrayed Sextus Pompeius into Antony's hands. After Actium his death sentence was commuted by Octavius.

Schoolmaster to Antony. *Antony and Cleopatra.* *And see* Evans, Holofernes, Pinch.

Scotland, King of. *See* Duncan, Macbeth, Malcolm.

Scroop (Scrope), Richard, archbishop of York, *c.* 1350-1405, supported Henry IV in 1399, but later joined with Northumberland in rebellion. In the play he gives no cogent reason for his action. Beheaded, he was venerated as a saint by the credulous people. *2 Henry IV.*

Scroop (Scrope), Sir Stephen. *Richard II.* He became lord Scroop, but joined Cambridge's conspiracy against Henry V, and was executed. *Henry V.*

Scrivener, a. *Richard III.*

Sea-captain, friend to Viola. *Twelfth Night.*

Seacole, George. *Much Ado About Nothing.*

Sebastian, brother to the king of Naples, shipwrecked with him on Prospero's island. *The Tempest.*

Sebastian, brother to Viola, saved from shipwreck, wins the hand of the countess Olivia. *Twelfth Night.*

Sebastian, name assumed by Julia. *The Two Gentlemen of Verona.*

Secretary. *Henry VIII.*

Seleucus, attendant on Cleopatra. *Antony and Cleopatra.*

Sempronius, false friend to Timon. *Timon of Athens.*

Sempronius, kinsman of Titus. *Titus Andronicus.*

Senators (a) Roman and Volscian, *Coriolanus.* (b) Roman, *Cymbeline, Julius Caesar, Titus Andronicus.*

Senators, in *Othello*, hold council with the Duke concerning the crisis in the Mediterranean with the advance of the Turks and give Othello command.

Senators, Four, in *Timon of Athens* join in embassy to him upon the sea-shore to persuade their former leading nobleman to return to the city in its peril from the enemy's approach. They offer him the captaincy – to be rejected, of course. The situation is rather like that of Coriolanus, whom Shakespeare was reading up in Plutarch about the same time.

Sergeant(s), *Macbeth*; French, *1 Henry VI.*

Sergeant-at-Arms, *Henry VIII, Sir Thomas More.*

Servant, the First, witnessing Gloucester's blinding by Cornwall, fatally wounds the miscreant. Thereupon Regan stabs him. *King Lear.*

Servants, in the house of Tullius Aufidius in *Coriolanus* have a part. They mistrust and bait the stranger, Coriolanus in disguise, until he beats them off. In this classic play without a sub-plot, citizens, senators, officers, soldiers, guards, conspirators, servants occupy its place, and contribute to the action.

Servants, amusing as usual. Induction to *The Taming of the Shrew.*

Servilius, servant of Timon. *Timon of Athens.*

Seton, officer attending on Macbeth, who brings news of Lady Macbeth's death. *Macbeth.*

Sexton, a. *Hamlet.*

Sexton, a. *Much Ado About Nothing.*

Sextus Pompeius, 75-35 BC, son of Pompey the Great, who carried on war against Octavius and Antony. In command of a large fleet he possessed himself of Sicily, and it needed great efforts to prise him out and defeat him. Fleeing to Asia Minor, he was captured and put to death. Appears in an amusing scene in *Antony and Cleopatra*: entertaining Antony on board ship, he makes him drunk but fails to overwhelm Octavius, the cooler head.

Shadow, Simon, Falstaff's recruit. *2 Henry IV.*

Shallow, Robert, a Gloucestershire Justice of the Peace in *2 Henry IV*. An endearing caricature of a somewhat senile country gentleman of the Cotswolds - such as Shakespeare observed at home there - with his nostalgic memories as a young fellow at the Inns of Court. Shallow - the name is indicative, as frequently with Shakespeare - is taken advantage of by Falstaff, with whom he appears again in *The Merry Wives of Windsor*.

Shepherd, Old (a) father of Joan of Arc. *1 Henry VI*. (b) Supposed father of Perdita. *The Winter's Tale*.

Sheriff(s), *1* and *2 Henry VI, King John, Richard III, Sir Thomas More*.

Sherwin, *Sir Thomas More*.

Shipmaster. *The Tempest*.

Shrewsbury, George Talbot, 4th earl, 1468-1538. *Sir Thomas More*.

Shylock, the rich Jew in *The Merchant of Venice* whose attempted exaction of a pound of flesh from the Merchant Antonio is the crux of the play. For us the play grazes upon the evil theme of anti-Semitism, so prominent today. Once more we see how relevant Shakespeare is to our time. The play begins with the stock Elizabethan caricature of the Jew, as with Marlowe's Barabbas; but before long Shakespeare's humanity breaks in: 'Hath not a Jew eyes? Hath not a Jew hands, organs, dimensions, senses, affections, passions?'

Today, our sympathies are with Shylock rather than with the Merchant, who had treated him with scorn, which motivated Shylock's revenge. Instead, he is balked of his bond, his possessions confiscated, even his daughter Jessica absconds to marry a Christian. We do not find that funny, as Elizabethans did. It redoubled his desire for revenge.

The play was sparked off - as was Shakespeare's way, with his eye on the box-office - by a contemporary event: the sensational case of Dr Lopez, his trial and execution -which Essex disgracefully urged forward - in 1594. This led to the revival of Marlowe's *The Jew of Malta*, and to Shakespeare's play in 1596.

The scene - with its harbour, wharves, Exchange, merchants venturing their argosies, dependent on wind and wave, liable to chance and loss - is of course Elizabethan London, as we see it rendered precisely in the consultations, exactly contemporaneously, of Forman.

It is thought that the Bassanos - like Lopez and Florio, Southampton's Italian tutor - were Jews; and Shakespeare's Dark Lady was a Bassano by birth. He was closer to the subject than has been realised, and knew well what he was writing about.

It is apropos of this play that Dr Johnson wisely remarks: 'I am always inclined to believe that Shakespeare has more allusions to particular facts and persons than his readers commonly suppose.' QED.

Sicilia, King of, *see* Leontes. *Also see* Hermione, Mamillius.

Sicilius, father of Leonatus Posthumus, appears in the masque. *Cymbeline.*

Sicinius Velutus (Belutus), tribune of the people who, with his fellow Junius Brutus, incites the mob against Coriolanus. Described by the wise Menenius as malicious. Thus Shakespeare again describes tribunes of the people. *Coriolanus.*

Silence, Shallow's cousin. *2 Henry IV.*

Silius, officer in Ventidius's army. *Antony and Cleopatra.*

Silvia, daughter of the duke of Milan, in *The Two Gentlemen of Verona.* Valentine is in love with her; but when his friend Proteus arrives he transfers his former love to Silvia, and betrays his friend. On his repentance, Valentine yields up Silvia to him:

> *All that was mine in Silvia I give thee.*

Improbable as this seems in the play, it is what happened when Shakespeare had to make way for his friend and patron with Emilia Lanier. The whole subject of the play is autobiographical.

Silvius, shepherd. *As You Like It.*

Simonides, king of Pentapolis, who gives his daughter, Thaisa, in marriage to Pericles. *Pericles.*

Simpcox, an imposter, and wife. *2 Henry VI.*

Simple, Peter, servant to Slender. *The Merry Wives of Windsor.*

Siward, earl of Northumberland, general of the English forces which overthrow Macbeth. *Macbeth.* Young Siward, his son.

Slender, Abraham, cousin to Justice Shallow. *The Merry Wives of Windsor.*

Sly, Christopher, the drunk tinker of the Induction to *The Taming of the Shrew*, who is made to believe that he is a lord, for whom the play proper is performed. Sly is old Sly's son of Barton-on-the-Heath (where Shakespeare's uncle and aunt lived, and the Induction has several references to his familiar surroundings at Stratford and in the Cotswolds).

Smith, weaver, one of Cade's rebels. *2 Henry VI.*

Snare, sergeant of the law. *2 Henry IV.*

Snout, Tom, tinker. *A Midsummer Night's Dream.*

Snug, joiner. *A Midsummer Night's Dream.*

Solanio, friend of Antonio the Merchant. *The Merchant of Venice.*

Solinus, *see* Ephesus.

Somerset, John Beaufort, earl then 1st duke, 1403-1444, son of John of Gaunt; briefly governed Aquitaine and Normandy for Henry VI. Opponent of Richard, duke of York. *1* and *2 Henry VI.*

Somerset, Edmund Beaufort, 2nd duke, younger brother of 1st duke. During his rule in France, as Lieutenant for Henry VI, most of the English possessions were lost. In the feud between Lancastrians and Yorkists he was killed at the first battle of St Albans. *2 Henry VI.*

Somerset, Henry Beaufort, 3rd duke, 1436-1464, son of the 2nd duke. He defeated the Yorkists at Wakefield and the second battle of St Albans. On Edward IV's capture of the Crown, Somerset supported Queen Margaret's opposition in the North, but was taken prisoner and executed at Hexham. *3 Henry VI.* These Somersets are not distinguished from each other in the trilogy.

Somervile, Sir John. *3 Henry VI.*

Son, that has killed his father. *3 Henry VI.*

Soothsayer, in *Antony and Cleopatra*, warns Antony not to take on Octavius, in fight or at any game: he is bound to lose.

> *He beats thee 'gainst the odds. Thy lustre*
> > *thickens*
> *When he shines by.*

He also tells the fortunes of Cleopatra's attendants.

Soothsayer, in *Cymbeline*, by name Philharmonus, interprets the oracle from Jupiter, which portends the happiness of Cymbeline and his issue (i.e. James I, his two sons and only daughter, as with Cymbeline. And how much the oracle was out! - for shortly after, in 1612, Prince Henry died, and think what happened to Charles I!).

Soothsayer in *Julius Caesar*, has the famous warning, 'Beware the Ides of March'; to which Caesar replies 'he is a dreamer', and takes no notice.

Soundpost, James, musician. *Romeo and Juliet.*

Southwell, John, priest. *2 Henry VI.*

Spanish Gentleman. *Cymbeline. See also* Armado.

Speed, servant to Valentine. *The Two Gentlemen of Verona.* His lower-class talk with his fellow-servant, Launce, provides the best fun in the play.

Spirits (a) appear to Queen Katharine. *Henry VIII.* (b) *The Tempest.*

Stafford, Sir Humphry and his brother William, slain in Cade's rebellion. *2 Henry VI.*

Stafford, Sir Humphry, a Yorkist, knighted by Edward IV
at Towton, 1461. *3 Henry VI.*
See also Buckingham.

Stanley, Sir John, knighted 1471. *2 Henry VI.*

Stanley, Sir William, knighted 1471. *3 Henry VI.*
See also Derby.

Starveling, Robin, tailor. *A Midsummer Night's Dream.*

Stephano, a drunken butler. *The Tempest.*

Stephano, servant to Portia. *The Merchant of Venice.*

Steward, to the Countess of Rousillon. *All's Well That Ends
Well.*
See also Flavius, Malvolio.

Strato, servant of Brutus. *Julius Caesar.*

Suffolk, William de la Pole, 4th earl and 1st duke,
1396-1450. Served in the war in France, on his return
forwarded a peace policy and arranged Henry VI's
marriage to Margaret of Anjou. Blamed for the cession
of Maine and Anjou, and highly unpopular, he was
banished and, caught in the Channel, was beheaded at
sea. A favourite of Queen Margaret, he was the enemy of
Richard of York. *1* and *2 Henry VI.*

Suffolk, Charles Brandon, duke of, d. 1545. *Henry VIII.*

Sugarsop. *The Taming of the Shrew.*

Surrey, Thomas Holland, duke, 1374-1400. Son of the 2nd
earl of Kent and Joan the 'Fair Maid of Kent', whose
second husband was the Black Prince. Richard II was his

147

half-brother. The son was an active supporter of the King, who made him duke of Surrey. Henry IV deprived him of the ducal title; Surrey revolted and was killed in the event. *Richard II.*

Surrey, Thomas Fitzalan, actually earl of Arundel and Surrey, 1381-1415, supported Henry IV, accompanied Henry V to France, took part in the siege of Harfleur, died on campaign. *2 Henry IV.*

Surrey, Thomas Howard, earl, became 2nd duke of Norfolk, fought for Richard III at Bosworth. *Richard III.*

Surrey, Thomas Howard, 1473-1554, earl, later 3rd duke of Norfolk, appears in Act II, 3 of *Sir Thomas More. Henry VIII.*

Surveyor, to the duke of Buckingham. *Henry VIII.*

Sycorax, mother of Caliban. *The Tempest.*

Tailor, a. *The Taming of the Shrew*.

Talbot, John, lord, 1st earl of Shrewsbury, *c.* 1384-1453.
Traditional hero of the war in France for dash and
daring, a folk bogey to the French; governed in
Normandy, fought in many actions, including the siege
of Orléans. Took Bordeaux; killed charging the cannon at
Castillon. *1 Henry VI.* cf. Nashe, 1592, 'How it would
have joyed brave Talbot, the terror of the French, to
think that, after he had lain 200 [actually 138] years in
his tomb, he should triumph again on the stage, and have
his bones new embalmed with the tears of 10,000
spectators at least, at several times, who in the tragedian
that represents his person imagine they behold him fresh
bleeding?' What a tribute to Shakespeare's earliest play!
No wonder Robert Greene was jealous.

Talbot, John, lord, son of 1st earl, killed with his father in
France. *1 Henry VI.*

Tamora, queen of the Goths, whom the Emperor Saturninus
marries. Titus Andronicus exacts the life of her son,
Alarbus, in return for the lives of his sons lost in war.
This sets going a chain of feuds in this early barbaric
play - probably Shakespeare's first, in which he was set
on out-doing Kyd's *Spanish Tragedy* in horrors
- all rather Grand Guignol to us, not to be taken too
seriously. Tamora cuckolds her husband with Aaron the

Moor, who gives her a black bastard. They all get their come-uppance horribly in the end. *Titus Andronicus.*

Tarsus, governor of. *See* Cleon.

Taurus, Statilius, lieutenant-general of Octavius, for whom he commanded the land forces at Actium. *Antony and Cleopatra.*

Tearsheet, Doll, Falstaff's whore, frequents the Boar's Head in East Cheap. *2 Henry IV.*

Thaisa, daughter of King Simonides in *Pericles*, who wins her hand at the Court of Pentapolis. In a storm at sea she gives birth to a daughter, Marina, and is presumed to have died. She survives, however, to become priestess of a temple at Ephesus where, after various wanderings and adventures, all three were reunited. The play appealed to Jacobean taste and was very successful, though we have only a poor memorial text of the first two Acts.

Thaliard, a lord of Antioch. *Pericles.*

Thersites, along with Ulysses the most interesting character in *Troilus and Cressida*. He serves the part of a Clown, and is beaten by Ajax - which would have been popular on stage with Elizabethans. Really he is a disillusioned and bitter cynic, commenting on the silliness of people's actions, in particular the Trojan war, caused by the abduction of Helen by Paris - though a common enough enterprise in primitive societies. He describes the epic conflict as merely a 'war for a placket' - a contemporary word for petticoat. He is a Swiftian character - much to be said for him.

Once more Dr Johnson noticed that here was a character which it gave Shakespeare pleasure to write:

'The comic characters seem to have been the favourites of the writer.' Few critics appreciate this. The great Doctor also perceived that this character, who does not appear in Caxton's Troy book - which Shakespeare mostly followed - 'is a proof that this play was written after Chapman had published his version of Homer'.

Theseus, duke of Athens, in *A Midsummer Night's Dream*, whose marriage to Hippolyta concludes the play. They are an elderly stately couple, in contrast to the young lovers who come in from maying, on Mayday, not midsummer. The play, conceived as a midsummer story (cf. Sonnet 98), was given this point to celebrate the private marriage of the elderly couple, Southampton's mother, the dowager Countess, and Sir Thomas Heneage, Vice-Chamberlain, on 2 May 1594.

Dr Johnson noticed the discrepancy. 'I know not why Shakespeare calls this play *A Midsummer Night's Dream*, when he so carefully informs us that it happened on the night preceding Mayday.' This is the answer.

Thidias, follower of Octavius. *Antony and Cleopatra*.

Thisbe, impersonated by Flute. *A Midsummer Night's Dream*.

Thump, Peter. *2 Henry VI*.

Thurio, gentleman of Milan, suitor to Silvia. *The Two Gentlemen of Verona*.

Timandra, one of Alcibiades' whores. *Timon of Athens*.

Time, as Chorus. *The Winter's Tale*.

Timon, the subject - one cannot say the hero - of *Timon of Athens*. Timon the Misanthrope was an historical figure who lived in the time of the Peloponnesian war. Disgusted with the ingratitude he experienced from friends, he withdrew from society. Shakespeare was particularly aware of ingratitude - here is his treatment of the subject; probably finding misanthropy an uncongenial subject, he did not finish the play.

From one extreme to the other - such a character was not sympathetic to William Shakespeare, who was all for moderation and prudence. Nor can we sympathise with Timon, throwing his substance away on extravagant liberality, profuse, ostentatious generosity. Apemantus, cynic philosopher - another version of Thersites in *Troilus and Cressida* - sums him up and faces Timon with the truth about himself. From too much trust in men he plunges into hatred, to pray the gods:

> And grant, as Timon grows, his hate may
> grow
> To the whole race of mankind, high and low.

At the end, digging for roots to live on, he finds gold. This reflects the mania for gold-digging - instead of planting - in Virginia at the time.

Titania, queen of the fairies. *A Midsummer Night's Dream.*

Titinius, follower of Brutus and Cassius. *Julius Caesar.*

Titus, servant of one of Timon's creditors. *Timon of Athens.*

Titus Andronicus, a noble old Roman who has deserved well of the state, but yields the throne the people wish him to take to Saturninus. He exacts the life of Tamora's son, queen of the Goths, in return for his sons' lives. Thus is

> ... her sacred wit
> To villainy and vengeance consecrate.

A chain of horrors is unleashed, in this early school-play,

with its Latin tags and classical references. The subject of *Titus Andronicus* is not historical, but comes from a medieval source.

Titus Lartius, general against the Volscians. *Coriolanus*.

Toby Belch, Sir. *See* Belch.

Tom (a) *1 Henry IV*. (b) *2 Henry VI*. (Poor Tom, name assumed by Edgar. *King Lear*.)

Topas, Sir, impersonated by Feste. *Twelfth Night*.

Touchstone, clown. *As You Like It*.

Tranio, servant to Lucentio. *The Taming of the Shrew*.

Travers, opponent of the King. *2 Henry IV*.

Trebonius, C., one of the conspirators in *Julius Caesar*. He had served under Caesar in Gaul, and when he was driven out of Spain by a mutiny, Caesar made him consul in 45 BC. Next year he joined the conspiracy. After Caesar's death, surprised at Smyrna he was slain in his bed.

Tressel, attendant on the Queen. *Richard III*.

Tribunes, Roman. *Coriolanus*. *Cymbeline*. *Julius Caesar*. *Titus Andronicus*.

Trinculo, jester, takes part in the conspiracy against Prospero. *The Tempest*.

Troilus, hero - if that is the word for it - of *Troilus and Cressida*. Son of Priam, king of Troy, he falls passionately in love with Cressida - but

I cannot come to Cressid but by Pandar.

He is her uncle, eggs the young man on and makes the
way clear. The lovers enjoy each other and swear eternal
vows. The young man is faithful to them, but is bitterly
disillusioned when he witnesses his Cressida - in the
Greek camp - transfer her favours as easily to another,
the Greek Diomedes. Thus Troilus:

O Cressid, O false Cressid, false, false, false!
Let all untruths stand by thy stainèd name.

The conclusion was traditional, but Shakespeare knew it
from personal experience.

Troy, King of. *See* Priam.

Tubal, friend of Shylock, with whom he exchanges
confidences as Jews. *The Merchant of Venice.*

Tullus (Tullius) Aufidius, leader of the Volscians
- historically he was their king - against the Romans in
Coriolanus. An enemy of that hero, he received him in
exile and gave him command against Rome. On his
sparing the city and returning to Volsci, Coriolanus paid
the penalty.

Tybalt, Lady Capulet's nephew, in *Romeo and Juliet,* a
quarrelsome, duelling swordsman, of whom there were
exemplars in Elizabethan England, let alone Italy.
Mercutio calls him 'Prince of Cats', a slur on his name.
He kills Mercutio, whose death Romeo avenges by
killing Tybalt, for which he is banished and wins the
execration of the Capulets. Mercutio dies with the
famous phrase, 'A plague on both your houses' on his
lips.

154

Tyrrell, Sir James. Master of the Horse to Richard III, for whom he arranged the murder of the Princes in the Tower. In spite of the secrecy that shrouded the matter he ultimately paid for the crime, confessing before his execution in 1502. *Richard III.*

Ulysses, Greek prince in *Troilus and Cressida*, the wisest and most sympathetic character, given the finest speeches, expressing Shakespeare's views on society and politics, government and the necessity of order - anarchy the alternative.

Ursula (a) attendant on Hero. *Much Ado About Nothing.* (b) *The Two Gentlemen of Verona.*

Urswick, Christopher, priest, 1448-1522. *Richard III.* Confessor to Henry VII, his mother and wife. An experienced diplomat, he negotiated Henry's marriage to Elizabeth, heiress of York - after the murder of her brothers in 1483 - and accompanied Henry to England in 1485. Dean of Windsor. *Richard III.*

Valentine, gentleman attending on the Duke. *Twelfth Night*.

Valentine, kinsman of Titus. *Titus Andronicus*.

Valentine, one of *The Two Gentlemen of Verona*, friend of Proteus, who betrays friendship, repents and is forgiven. Thereupon Valentine gives up his girl, Silvia, to the offender. This *dénouement* has always been regarded as improbable and unconvincing. It is in fact precisely what happened when Shakespeare had to give way to his young friend and patron over Emilia Lanier - the Dark Lady of the Sonnets, which parallel and completely corroborate that the inspiration of the play was autobiographical. It had no other source.

Valeria, friend of Coriolanus's wife. An amusing gossip, she brings a breath of contemporary realism and a bit of light relief into this austere and classic play. *Coriolanus*.

Varrius, attendant on the Duke. *Measure for Measure*.

Varrius, follower of Sextus Pompeius. *Antony and Cleopatra*.

Varro, servant to Brutus. *Julius Caesar*.

Vaughan, Sir Thomas. A faithful Yorkist, yet executed by Richard III for loyalty to young Edward V. *Richard III*.

157

Vaux. *2 Henry VI.*

Vaux, Sir Nicholas. Became 1st lord, d. 1523. *Henry VIII.*

Venice, duke of, before whom comes Shylock's case against the Merchant. *The Merchant of Venice.*

Venice, duke of, who gives Othello command against the Turks in Cyprus. *Othello.*

Ventidius, friend of Timon. *Timon of Athens.*

Ventidius, (Bassus P.), friend of Antony. *Antony and Cleopatra.* Historically, a rare case of a man who rose from the ranks to become a general. He did so well against the Parthians that Antony, jealous of his success, dismissed him.

Verges, a head-borough, i.e. petty-constable, companion of the inimitable Dogberry. *Much Ado About Nothing.*

Vernon, Sir Richard. *1 Henry IV.*

Vernon, a Yorkist. *1 Henry VI.*

Vincentio, duke. *See* Duke.

Vincentio, merchant of Pisa. *The Taming of the Shrew.*

Vintner. *1 Henry IV.*

Viola, sister to Sebastian in *Twelfth Night.* Disguised as a youth, she is the Duke's intermediary in his suit to the Countess Olivia, who falls for her as such. Olivia is eventually provided more suitably with Sebastian, the Duke with Viola.

Violenta, friend to the widow of Florence. *All's Well That Ends Well.*

Virgilia is named in *Coriolanus* as his wife, who traditionally was Volumnia, the name given here to his mother. A passive female, she stands in some contrast to her steely mother-in-law.

Voltemand, courtier. *Hamlet.*

Volumnia, mother of the hero in *Coriolanus*, classic image of a Roman matron. She had brought him up hard and was responsible for his fate, by persuading him to spare his native city, after it had spewed him out. Much admired as a character, is she altogether sympathetic? Not to me.

Volumnius, friend of Brutus and Cassius. *Julius Caesar.*

Wales, Princes of, *see* Edward, Henry.

Wall, impersonated by Snout. *A Midsummer Night's Dream*.

Walter. *The Taming of the Shrew*.

Warders. *1 Henry VI. Sir Thomas More*.

Warham, William, archbishop of Canterbury. *Henry VIII*.

Wart, Falstaff's recruit. *2 Henry IV*.

Warwick, Edward Plantagenet, earl, 1475-1499. Son of George, duke of Clarence, executed by Henry VII. *Richard III*.

Warwick, Richard Beauchamp, earl, 1382-1439. Accompanied Henry V to France, where he held commands, culminating as Lieutenant ruling for Henry VI. Died at Rouen, buried in a splendid tomb with effigy at St Mary's, Warwick. *2 Henry IV, Henry V, 1 Henry VI*.

Warwick, Richard Neville, earl, 1428-1471. Married daughter and heiress of Richard Beauchamp. Yorkist leader, he was Edward IV's right-hand man, until offended by the King's marriage. Went over to Henry VI, whom he restored - thus his soubriquet, 'the king-maker'. Killed at Barnet. *3 Henry VI*.

Watchmen, two, in *Much Ado About Nothing*, witnesses to Borachio's exposure.

Watchmen, Chief, Second, Third. *Romeo and Juliet.*

Westminster, abbot of. *Richard II.*

Westmorland (a) Ralph Neville, 1st earl, 1364-1425, a supporter of Richard II; sensibly went over to Henry IV. *1 and 2 Henry IV.* (b) Ralph Neville, 2nd earl; d. 1484. *3 Henry VI.*

Whitmore, Walter, one of Suffolk's murderers. *2 Henry VI.*

Widow, a. *The Taming of the Shrew.*

Widow of Florence, a, who agrees to the bed-trick by which Count Bertram is enticed into bed with his wife. *All's Well That Ends Well.*

Will. *2 Henry VI.*

William, a simple country fellow. *As You Like It.*

Williams, Michael, soldier in Henry V's army. *Henry V.*

Williamson, a carpenter and wife, Doll. *Sir Thomas More.*

Willoughby, William, 5th lord, *c.* 1370-1409. *Richard II.* He has a splendid brass, with his 1st wife, at Spilsby, Lincs.

Wiltshire, sheriff of. *Richard III.*

Winchester, bishops of. *See* Beaufort, Gardiner.

Witches, the Three, in *Macbeth*. What are we to think of these horrible hags, their imprecations and their

161

prophecies? They have a decisive effect on Macbeth, when their prophecy that he will become Thane of Cawdor immediately comes true. It corroborates his ambition to become king and urges him to make that come true. They also prophesy that his companion, Banquo, shall be the ancestor of a long line – the Stuarts.

Dr Johnson, to whom the subject of superstition was congenial, devoted most of his commentary on this play to the question. He sees it properly in historical terms, contemporary with Shakespeare. 'In order to make a true estimate of the abilities and merit of a writer, it is always necessary to examine the genius of his age, and the opinions of his contemporaries ... He only turned the system that was then universally admitted to his advantage, and was far from overwhelming the credulity of his audience. The reality of witchcraft ... has in all ages and countries been credited by the common people, and in most by the learned themselves ... Upon this general infatuation Shakespeare might be easily allowed to found a play, especially since he has followed with great exactness such histories as were then thought true. Nor can it be doubted that the scenes of enchantment were both by himself and his audience thought awful and affecting.' *Verb. sap.*

Witches, Three Other, along with Hecate, classical goddess of the underworld, were added to *Macbeth*, probably by Middleton, to increase the supernatural effect. But in conflict with Shakespeare's scheme; for there is nothing classical about this Northern, Gothick play.

Wolsey, Thomas, ?1475–1530, Henry VIII's chief minister for many years before his fall in 1529. Of immense ability and ambition, he was a glutton for work and everything. He served the King loyally, also ministering to his pleasures, for Wolsey had a charm in his tongue. But, though a cardinal and a European figure, he could not procure from the Pope Henry's divorce from Katharine of Aragon to marry Anne Boleyn. In a blind alley with no way out, his policies bankrupt, Wolsey was dismissed from Court to his archbishopric of York. Summoned ominously back for investigation, he died on the way at Leicester abbey. A patron of art and learning, a would-be reformer, he set the example of suppressing redundant monasteries to found Christ Church, Oxford, and a big school at Ipswich, which unfortunately fell with him. A leading character, a favourite part with famous actors, in *Henry VIII*.

Woodville, Lieutenant of the Tower of London. *1 Henry VI*.

Worcester, Thomas Percy, earl of, 1343-1403, brother of 1st earl of Northumberland. Supported Henry IV's call to the throne, but revolted and joined his nephew, Hotspur, at Shrewsbury; after which he was beheaded. *1 Henry IV*. These Percies should have been contented with what they had got for supporting Bolingbroke.

York, archbishop of. *Richard III*. Thomas Rotherham, 1423-1500.

And see Wolsey.

York, Edmund of Langley, 1st duke of, 1341-1402, 5th son of Edward III, the least able of them all. Regent during Richard II's absence, he went over to Bolingbroke's side on his return to claim his rights. By his first wife he had two sons, Edward, one of Richard II's 'duketti' as Duke of Aumerle, and Richard, earl of Cambridge. York's second wife was Joan Holland, who has an effective part in *Richard II*. Shakespeare treats this Duchess as Aumerle's mother, whereas she was his stepmother.

York, Edward, 2nd duke of, killed at Agincourt, 1415. *Henry V*.

York, Richard, 3rd duke, 1411-1460, son of Richard, earl of Cambridge, and Anne Mortimer. Through the female line he was descended from Edward III's third son, hence his claim to the throne. Henry VI's incapacity and mental illness led him to put it forward. He was bitterly opposed by Queen Margaret and her party, the Lancastrian Beauforts. Henry VI agreed to a compromise by which York should succeed him, but he was killed at a skirmish near Wakefield, his head displayed on the walls of York disdainfully crowned with a paper crown. *2 and 3 Henry VI*.

York, duchess of, Cecily Neville, wife of 3rd duke, and mother of Edward IV, Clarence, and Richard III. A pious lady, she was much grieved by Richard's dishonouring her in declaring his brother Edward IV illegitimate. *Richard III.*

York, Richard, duke of, 1472-1483, Edward IV's son, murdered by Richard III. *Richard III.*

York, mayor of. *3 Henry VI.*

Young Cato, in *Julius Caesar*, follower of Brutus and Cassius, fell at Philippi. He was the son of the famous Stoic, the subject of Addison's *Cato*, on whom George Washington modelled his republican image.

Young Lucius, son of Titus's son, Lucius. *Titus Andronicus.*

Young Martius, Coriolanus's son. *Coriolanus.*

Young Siward, son of Siward, earl of Northumberland, slain by Macbeth at Dunsinane. *Macbeth.*

Young Talbot, *see* Talbot.